The Storms As They Roll In

Anchored by Faith

Maureen Rose Morley

Finch and Squirrel LLC

Copyright © 2025 Finch and Squirrel LLC

All rights reserved.

No portion of this book may be reproduced in any form without written permission from the publisher or author, except as permitted by U.S. copyright law.

ISBN: 978-1-7340258-9-7

Cover design by Yonathan K.

Finch and Squirrel LLC

www.finchandsquirrel.com

Contents

Foreword	VII
Introduction	XI
1. The Storms As They Roll In	1
The Road to Vancouver	4
2. My Narnia	10
3. Traveling Mercies	12
4. My Church Family	16
5. Acting In	18
6. My Bald Head	21
7. Oh Lord I'll Try	24
8. A Turning Point	28
9. Help Me, Please	37
10. A Big Comfy Chair	39
11. I'm Okay	42
12. I Think Too Much	45

13.	Praying for Time	47
14.	An American Thanksgiving in Canada	50
15.	Strength Solid and Enduring	55
16.	Men and Women in the Kingdom of God	57
17.	I Have to Write a Will	60
18.	Take a Deep Breath	67
19.	An Army of Aches and Pains	71
20.	We Need a Vacation	75
21.	A Wild Place	84
22.	Not a Tragedy	89
23.	Epilogue	97

Foreword

By Therese Simpson

"Hope" is the illegible word etched into a simple silver band I wear on my left thumb. I bought it the week my sister, Maureen Rose Morley, found out that her breast cancer had metastasized to her bones.

I'll never forget the call. Mo, as many of us fondly called her, had moved a few months earlier from the little cottage where she lived not far from me in Warrenton, Virginia, to Vancouver, British Columbia. Having accepted Jesus Christ as her savior, she felt the call to sell her home and most of her belongings and pursue a master's degree in Christian Studies at Regent College.

The youngest girl in our family, the ninth of ten children born to our parents, Maureen was quiet and dainty, with an ethereal sweetness, unlike me, the sister closest to her in age. She spent her days with her nose in a book while I, rambunctious and full of energy, ran amok in the woods. We were not close as children but developed a beautiful friendship as young women, after I surrendered my life to Jesus Christ. Maureen saw the change in me and began to accompany me to church and to Bible study, and eventually came with me to a women's retreat, where she too accepted Christ as her savior.

Before devoting her life to Christ, Maureen would not have described herself as a happy person. She once admitted to me that she was "used to living at high-level sad." She would sigh a lot, as if she couldn't quite take in enough breath.

All of that changed after Maureen gave her life to Jesus Christ. She had long been a seeker, with a lively, curious mind and a love of learning. After graduating from college, she pursued a doctorate in psychology but became disillusioned with the program when she felt it was missing something essential. Eventually she discovered what that missing piece was: Maureen couldn't imagine healing people without the "Spirit." That was when she set out in search of the Spirit and the Truth.

When she found Jesus Christ, Maureen was instantly filled with His spirit. I remember seeing her take a deep breath and then give a long exhale. Her body relaxed. Her countenance changed. She had met God and had received a love greater than anything she had experienced before. The sadness that had gripped her for years was replaced with a quiet joy. For the rest of her life, she walked in grace and kindness, showing the world what the love of Christ looked like. Maureen was an angel on this earth.

Her deepest desire was for all to know Christ, and that is what compelled her to write so prolifically in her final years. "I don't want to write for an audience," Maureen said. "I want to write for the sake of the truth. But one reason to write is simply to bear witness. Maybe that is more to the point of what I am doing. God has done something in my life. I do want to bear witness to that."

Maureen passed peacefully before she could complete her work. Among her final wishes, she asked her husband, Steve Morley, to pass her writing to our sister Barbara, along with her permission to share it. What follows is a collection of essays, prayers, and stories that chronicle Maureen's evolving faith in the face of a terminal diagnosis. Through her writing, she shares her walk with Jesus on Earth.

Sometimes she is speaking to herself, sometimes to us, the readers. She shares conversations with friends and family; she appeals to God and asks urgent questions. She speaks of the books that gave her hope as a child and inspired her as an adult and aspiring author. She takes us into the room with her cancer group. She introduces us to the love of her life, her husband Steve, whom she met in Vancouver, and her dreams for their life together. She shares her worries and concerns and the sorrow of knowing the pain those who loved her would experience when she left this world.

Years later, as she knew we would, we miss her deeply. It is, however, a comfort to know that Maureen is living in eternity with Jesus her savior. Maureen would want you to know Jesus too, and we offer you the gift of the words she set down on paper and their messages of hope and love. We invite you to take a long, deep breath, exhale, open your heart, and turn the page.

Introduction

By Steve Morley

It was early June. I had moved to Vancouver nine months earlier to study theology at Regent Bible College on the University of British Columbia campus. Like all good theology students, I had found a local church, and this bright Sunday morning I walked into church, found my friend Adrian and sat next to him. Maureen was sitting on her own in the pew ahead of us; she had just moved to Vancouver to attend the same college. It was the first time I saw her.

After the service ended, Maureen turned 'round to say hello to the strangers in the pew behind her. She was pretty and slim, about my height, with shoulder length brown hair and blue/grey (but mostly blue) eyes. But the thing I noticed most was the frumpy blue denim dress Maureen wore. It didn't flatter her either in shape or colour. Little did I know it was her sister's dress, and wearing it was Maureen's way of feeling connected to family in a time of new beginnings.

I don't recall there being a spark of attraction between us at that first meeting. I think the blue denim dress put me off. Besides, in the time I had been at Vancouver I had already had my fingers burned. My English approach to dating had met with North American cross-cultural differences, and I was cautious of any woman who had girlfriend potential.

Having started college almost a year later than I, Maureen and I had different student social circles, but there was contact at church most Sundays and we had Adrian as a mutual friend. Adrian is one of those guys that every social group needs, the person who organises events and connects everyone together and lets them know when and where to meet. And all this before smartphones, Facebook, WhatsApp or other social media. He has a heart for a lost soul and made sure Maureen was invited to many of the social gatherings our group of friends attended.

A month after she arrived, I had to move out of one apartment and into another. I had a large van worth of personal belongings to move, but no van. Someone had told me that Maureen had lent her truck to another student for his move, and I was struck by her generosity. That was the thing you noticed about her. She held onto possessions and things lightly, and was generous. Really generous, without expecting anything back.

Maureen's truck was a sky blue, bright and shiny Ford Ranger with an extended cab and enclosed hood. A small truck in North America but a large vehicle by British standards. I asked to borrow the truck, and Maureen said yes without any hesitation. That was when I started to wonder about dating Maureen. Her external beauty was clear to see. But her inner beauty was starting to shine out, and I found that incredibly attractive.

June turned to July and July to August. Maureen and I continued to see each other in social settings, always with others present: at Bard on the Beach, at the pub, playing volleyball down on the shore overlooking English Bay, having coffee and cinnamon buns in Grounds for Coffee.

Never alone, never one to one, but something started to brew over those three months. I awakened out of my "I'm not going to date" slumber and, as she later told me, Maureen was "beginning to realise her femaleness again." At the beginning of August I got wind that another student had invited Maureen to dinner. He was older than she was by 10 years and, to my mind, completely unsuitable for her. I realised I needed to act or I was going to miss out and enter the dreaded "friend zone." To complicate matters, Maureen flew home to Virginia in August for three weeks to catch up with family before the new semester started in earnest in September. Adrian reminded me recently that towards the end of those three weeks, I confessed to him that I was missing Maureen.

By the time Maureen returned to Vancouver, we had independently come to the decision to take action. She got in first. It was the third of September, and a bunch of us were having afternoon coffee in the college atrium. It was the week before the semester started properly and Maureen asked if anyone wanted to come with her to get their student card for the year. Some had already got theirs and said no. I still needed to get mine, so without trying to appear too eager and as casually as I could manage, I said, "Sure, I will come with you." To both our disappointment a mutual friend, Kat, also said she would come.

The three of us walked the 25 minutes across campus to the student union building and waited in our alphabetical lines to get our student cards. Leary and Morley (L and M) were part of the same line and I had my first chance to speak with Maureen one to one. Kat must have picked up the vibe that Maureen and I wanted to be alone, because when we turned 'round to her line to look for her, she had already left.

What to do next? I asked Maureen if she had ever been to the rose garden on campus, to which she replied no. Neither had I, but I had been told by Adrian that it was a lovely place, with views overlooking the waters of English Bay and in the distance the shore of North Vancouver. We walked slowly towards the rose garden. It was still summer with a bright blue sky, sun shining overhead and no clouds. I had no idea that Rose was Maureen's middle name and roses were her favourite flower.

We were talking all the way to the garden. I took the lead, getting lost a few times, but the signs pointing to "Rose Garden" eventually led to a bench amidst a colour of red, orange, yellow and white roses. Some were starting to fade at the end of summer, but many were still vibrant, and from time to time the gentle breeze would waft a scent of rose perfume our way. I couldn't have come up with a more romantic setting or moment if I tried.

I understood that, with Maureen, if we started dating, there would be no messing about. We were both old enough to have got past the stage of dating for fun. As we sat among the roses and gazed out at the sea, alone in the rose garden, we talked about many things, but gradually I turned the conversation around to what we wanted to do after college and started to tell her my vision for life.

I was studying for a Master of Divinity and training to be a church pastor. It meant I would be working every Sunday; having a house which was open and hospitable to strangers and church members; attending church meetings two to four nights a week. I didn't say outright that I wanted a partner and spouse who was not only okay with this, but who would actively support me in the role. I was foolishly trying to paint as difficult a picture as I could so Maureen would know what she would be getting into if we dated and got married. I wanted to make sure she could never come back to me and say, "You didn't tell me it was going to be like this."

She sat there and listened to me describe how difficult the pastoral life could be, and her face didn't register an ounce of emotion. I had no idea that inside she was thinking, "This sounds really exciting, I could be a part of it." This was all part of courtship in the old sense of the word: Getting to know each other, sharing visions and dreams, but not yet ready to be open and fully vulnerable with each other.

The time crept 'round to late afternoon, and we walked slowly back to college, enjoying each other's company as the conversation turned towards more mundane things such as which courses we were going to take in the fall semester. Neither wanted the afternoon to end, but it was too soon for me to suggest we go on to dinner somewhere. Both of us needed to eat in our own homes and pause to reflect on what had just happened between us. After being acquainted for three months, we had had our first time alone together, and it had gone really well.

A few days later, Adrian rang to see if I wanted to go out to the cinema that evening with a group of students. I mentioned the rose garden conversation to him and he said Maureen was also coming out that evening. He suggested I call her and get her to give me a lift to the cinema. Around 7:00 p.m. Maureen was ringing my doorbell. When I opened the door, Maureen was standing at the top of the steps, and my jaw dropped to the floor. For the first time since I had known her, Maureen had put on makeup and jewelry and was dressed to impress in a red cotton blouse with elbow-length sleeves and a dark denim knee-length skirt with matching shoes in a slight heel. She looked stunning. I thought my jaw-drop had gone unnoticed, but a few months later she told me that she had noticed my look of amazement. Her plan had worked.

We got into her truck and she drove us to the cinema to meet up with the eight others. My game plan was simple: I would engage Maureen in conversation all the way through the ticket-buying stage, and we would be left with no choice but to sit next to each other for the whole of the movie. I think Maureen wanted that too, but I was taking no chances with any of our friends randomly coming between us. I never discussed this with Adrian, but he ran interference for me and herded all the others ahead of us. Maureen and I sat next to each other.

The movie was Bruce Almighty. There's a big risk in taking ten theology students to watch a movie where God gives all his powers to a random undeserving TV reporter. But the writing was excellent and the performances by Jim Carrey and Morgan Freeman were so good that I laughed my head off. At one point I got worried that Maureen would be put off by my loud laughter and all the scenes that triggered my outbursts. What I didn't know was that she was thinking to herself, "Good, Steve has a sense of humour and is not afraid to show it."

After the movie we all moved on to a local pub. It was one of those Central Perk type of setups you see in the TV show "Friends." I was sitting on one end of a couch, and Maureen sat opposite me. There were ten of us that night, but other than Adrian, I can't recall who else was there; I couldn't even tell you who was sitting next to me on the couch. Maureen and I just carried on from the rose garden three days earlier, talking and listening to each other. I had an early start the next day but was reluctant to leave until she did.

Finally it got to closing time. A few had drifted off already. Of the rest of us, Maureen had to drive right past my apartment on her way home, so she offered me a lift and of course I accepted. As we were getting into her truck, I was thinking it was time to raise the ante and be a bit clearer that my intentions were more than wanting just a friendship. Before I knew it, we had pulled up to the curb outside my house, and it was time to get out. Spontaneity hit me. I thanked her for the lift and wonderful evening, undid my seatbelt and leaned over and kissed her gently on the cheek. Then without a word, I opened my door and got out. Before closing the door, I leaned in to see her reaction which again I couldn't read. With a large grin on my face I said goodnight, closed the door, waved goodbye and entered my apartment.

"Right then, Steve," I said to myself, "You've given her something to think about." A few months after we started dating I asked Maureen about that goodbye moment and kiss. She said she could remember the big grin on my face and that made her smile. The kiss was, in her words, "Unexpected but not unwelcome." We both agreed that the whole evening had felt more like a date than part of a group of friends going out to a movie and a drink afterwards.

Over the summer I had got myself a regular crewing position on a J24 sailboat, and the next day I was scheduled to sail in a two-day regatta run by the Royal Vancouver Yacht Club. On this Saturday I was at Royal Van by 9:00 a.m., and we didn't finish until 5:00. The usual practice after racing is to go up to the club bar for a few beers before heading home, then repeat the next day. But the night before I had kissed Maureen on the cheek, I had raised the ante and realised too late that my weekend diary was full with racing. I wouldn't have a chance to see Maureen before college started on Monday. The last thing I wanted was to get to college, bump into each other between classes and try to find some private space on the first day of term to discuss how we felt about each other.

So, after sailing that Saturday, I rang Maureen and asked when she would be free to meet up. She had people over for dinner that night. She was free tomorrow, Sunday, in the daytime. But I would be in the middle of English Bay on a sailboat. She wasn't free Sunday evening. We left it that if her dinner party finished early enough that Saturday evening, Maureen would call me and we would meet up.

I went back to the bar, had a few beers, then went home, ate dinner and was busy telling myself to be more careful about timing in the future when the phone rang. It was 9:00 p.m. and Maureen's guests had just left, so she was free for the rest of the evening. I didn't have a car, and as she had transport, she said she could come over in about 20 minutes.

I didn't have a stove or electric kettle, so in preparation for her arrival, I put a saucepan of water on the stove to heat up for hot drinks. This time I was going to be properly prepared. Maureen arrived and suggested she drive us back to her apartment as she had to clear up from her dinner party. Would I mind coming over and we could talk while she cleaned up? I was happy just to be in her company. I didn't really care what we did. So I offered to dry dishes if she washed. We jumped into her truck and she drove back to her apartment. Neither of us mentioned the kiss the night before. At first it was a little awkward and the free-flowing conversation of the rose garden was replaced by polite enquiry about our days.

When we got to Maureen's apartment, she offered to make me a hot drink, and I remembered the saucepan of water I had put on the gas stove in my own apartment, which by now would be boiling away. And after the water evaporated, the fire would start to burn the pan and quite possibly my apartment and the whole house, including my landlady upstairs.

Quite sheepishly, I told Maureen about the impending fire hazard I had left unattended, which would be leading towards a fire crew being summoned to the scene and my face appearing on the local news as the culprit of a house fire in West Point Grey. She graciously agreed to drive me back to my house. I removed the saucepan of boiling water, turned off the gas, and we returned to Maureen's apartment to start all over again.

The ridiculous nature of the situation, the back and forth in her truck – I had lost count of how many journeys she made that evening – all worked to pop the tension we were experiencing, and we just laughed and laughed at the silliness of the situation. About midnight Maureen drove me home. This time she got out of her truck and walked me to my door. I turned to give her a hug – it was long as she hugged me back. Not too tight, but close and meaningful. That hug said "I am serious about this and serious about you." I kissed her again, this time on the lips, and said goodnight, watching as she got back into her truck and drove off before I went down into my basement apartment.

The next morning I was back at Royal Van, sailboat racing in light winds. After my seventh mistake in the first hour, my skipper asked me if I was alright because my mind didn't seem to be on the task at hand. It wasn't. My head was full of Maureen and the night before, but I wasn't about to admit that. I mumbled something about having too many beers the night before and apologised for my errors. My skipper was a generous man and, as this was my first bad day on his boat, he let it go.

I never did formally ask Maureen to go out with me. That Friday night at the cinema and Saturday night back and forth between our two apartments just cemented what had begun over the summer. It became clear we were dating when we walked into college hand in hand a week later and could be found sitting next to each other at church every Sunday.

By mid-term break we were inseparable. My brother was getting married in England and I was flying home during the break. A few weeks beforehand I messaged Simon and asked him if I could bring a plus one. Maureen agreed to come with me. I didn't know it at the time, but this trip to England was a test. It was over a nine-hour flight from Vancouver to London, and she reasoned that, if we could talk and not be bored with each other during a nine-hour flight, then a permanent future and marriage was possible. I didn't know I was being tested, but by the end of the trip she let it be known to me that if I proposed she would say yes.

We were barely two months on from that first kiss on the cheek. Even though there had been nothing that made me hesitate and everything said this woman is the real deal, I had an internal rule which said "No decisions until we have dated for three months." That three-month anniversary was fast approaching, and I couldn't see anything that would get in the way of me asking her to marry me. All was going so well. Then we got the health news that no couple ever wants to hear.

But that is Maureen's story. It's time for you, the reader, to turn the page and read it in her own words.

The Storms As They Roll In

2005

When the sky darkens with an approaching storm and sudden gusts of wind rush through the airways along the sides of my apartment building in Vancouver, I sometimes notice the eagles. Last August, longing for light, all it took was one look out these floor-to-ceiling west-facing windows for my husband Steve and me to know that we'd found our new home. When we moved in, we arranged the furniture for optimum outside views. As my friend Connie from the hospital support group says, these days are full of sitting and thinking and looking out windows.

Beyond my window, a huge fir tree moves slowly back and forth in the wind. I lift my eyes to the open air beyond, where I see the eagles. At the first glimpse of a speck of white on a big black bird body, I stop what I'm doing to watch. It is more than their bald heads that distinguishes these eagles from the crows that dwell in the nearby forest. The eagles' wide-spread wings seldom flap. They catch the air, and they soar, the gusts of wind their playground in the air. They soar boldly up, up, up into the currents, catch the wind-waves and ride, the picture of joyful abandon.

I'm inspired. I'd like to fly out to meet the storms as they roll in.

My life's search has led me to a place of recognizing that God is absolutely good and absolutely essential for my – and all of humankind's – greatest good.

With heart-rending sadness, I witness a seemingly endless number of misconceptions about who God is, and consequently who we human beings are, and these are just the ones I recognize. Misconceptions exist among both professing Christians and non-Christians. These misconceptions cause an endless supply of painful struggle in our lives, often keeping us from the relationship with God, through Jesus Christ, that is the most profound longing of our hearts.

I seek, then, to try in my own little way in my writing, to chip away at some of these misconceptions through exploration of and reflection upon what I have encountered through my experiences with myself and others – including both direct interpersonal interaction with people and reading what other people have written – and hearing directly from God himself through the Bible, prayer and other people. I hope that, as a result of this chipping away, a vision of God might begin to emerge that is closer to the truth than the many false conceptions that exist.

It is true that no conceptualization will explain God to us, his human creations who live here in space and time. I am dependent on language to communicate, and even if I were a master of language – which, it will be obvious, I am not – no analogy can capture him. And, of course, there must be a great deal that I understand wrongly. Yet, I believe that God in his bigness can get through even to puny me. He has gone to great lengths to reveal much about himself to us, and I trust him enough to imagine that what he tells us in his ongoing creative work is precisely what we need to know.

My desire is to join God in this work, as countless people have done through the ages. Dependent wholly upon the power of God's Spirit to do so, I add my voice to theirs.

The Road to Vancouver

2003

Mom snapped a picture of Barbara and me just before we headed off on our cross-country drive, 3,000 miles from Warrenton, Virginia, to Vancouver, British Columbia. This was minutes after my brother Steve and brother-in-law Jeff managed to cram closed and lock the U-Haul door over the full load of boxes and furniture it would carry behind my little royal blue Ford pick-up. In the picture, we're both dressed for the duration: sweat pants, t-shirts, baseball caps. In the background, Therese and the kids stood watching.

We hugged our goodbyes, and I waved off Jeff's last attempts to instruct me in how to reverse the truck when the U-Haul trailer is attached.

"Our goal is to not have to reverse at all during this trip," I said, looking to Barbara. She nodded a hearty assent. We started up the truck and pulled slowly away from the house.

This was going to be fun. There are few people with whom I can envision enjoying a drive across North America in five days, but Barbara is top of the list. She has a good sense of humor, likes to have fun, and is easy to talk with, smart and thoughtful. But she doesn't have to talk all the time. Sometimes, she borders on brooding, which suits me fine. I do my share. And she's not easily rattled. Best of all, I'm convinced she really likes me, as I do her. All these things made her a secure choice for a traveling companion.

It was Sunday when we left, and we decided to drive to the far side of Chicago before turning in for the night. After driving through Virginia, Maryland, Pennsylvania, Ohio and Indiana we made it to Illinois. We stopped for the night somewhere near Racine, close to Interstate 94, which we decided we'd pick up the next day. Our plan was to take the northernmost interstate route in the United States, all the way to Washington State. After thirteen hours on the road, Day One was completed successfully.

The next day took us through Wisconsin to Minnesota and on to North Dakota. Neither of us had ever driven this far north. The terrain became increasingly stark and expansive: plains. Neither of us relished the idea of another thirteen-hour day, so we stopped after more eight hours in Fargo, North Dakota. We chuckled at the Dakota accents at dinner, pleased to be in Fargo, the setting for the popular movie. I think we had salads, burgers and beers before heading off to bed for the night.

On Day Three, we drove through the Badlands of North Dakota, bare orange rock faces of forlorn beauty and odd shapes. This might have been the day when Barbara decided that she wanted pie. It seemed fitting. We were driving across America, and pie is a very American sort of thing. As exit after highway exit sped by without a likely prospect for pie, we lamented that we didn't have enough time to drive the smaller highways of the country. Surely the roads that linked little town after little town would be full of quirky dilapidated diners serving roast beef suppers and, for dessert, lots of homemade pie.

By now, I was driving and had caught Barbara's pie fever. "We're going to find some pie!" I said.

Moments later, we spotted the billboard for a restaurant coming up at the next exit: "Homemade Pie!" it promised.

I, for one, said a prayer of thanks to God for caring for us in both big and small ways. How delightful that we should run smack into this restaurant at just this time. There's been too much that has happened in my life for me to attribute anything to coincidence.

So Barbara and I stopped at the diner for lunch and finished it off with pie that turned out to be good but not spectacular, and continued on our way to our next stop, near Billings, Montana.

On Day Four, we had a similar experience in which I felt cared for by God. This time, it wasn't pie we wanted, but music: A place where we could buy a new CD. As it happened, our first pit stop led us straight to a Barnes and Noble bookstore. That night, we stayed in beautiful Coeur d'Alene, Idaho, near the border to Washington State.

So it was on Day Five of our trip that we drove north up Highway 5 in Washington State toward the Canadian border. By this time we were tired of driving and ready to arrive at our destination, but were buoyed by sight of the mountains that flanked us to the right and stood at attention in front of us as we approached the border.

When we reached the border, I realized I'd never had to clear customs by car. I felt a bit of a panic. Was I allowed to bring into the country everything I had with me? We had a couple bottles of alcohol. Could I bring that in? I found myself lying to the customs agent, answering "No," to his question about whether we had any alcohol, good honest Christian girl that I am. As the agent waved us through to immigration, we saw a customs agent standing by as a couple unloaded their belongings from a rented truck and felt relieved not to have been singled out for such treatment.

"You could have just told him 'yes' about the liquor, Mo. We're allowed to bring it into the country," said Barbara, bemused.

Our edginess was replaced by excitement and a decided sense of accomplishment when, less than an hour later, we were turning down the street of the house in Vancouver where I would be staying in the basement apartment.

But, uh-oh, it looked like a dead-end street, with no area to park in the direction we were heading. We would have to turn around. Yikes. After driving 3,000 miles without once putting the truck in reverse, must we now risk backing up? I drove down to the end of the street, and upon seeing the cul-de-sac, Barbara and I both chuckled. No backing up would be necessary. We pulled around and parked across the street from my new home.

We fished out the key the landlady had left for us and went around back to my private entrance. We decided to bring in just a few things from the U-Haul before relaxing for the evening.

But when we tried to roll up the U-Haul door, it refused to budge. I pulled little harder. Barbara pushed me aside and pulled. We both yanked up on the door handle together. I went in search of help and found a man working in his yard. He pulled and pulled, but soon gave up and left. "Our brothers wouldn't have given up," muttered Barbara.

Barbara was inclined to give up the attempt for the evening. Who could blame her? We'd come 3,000 miles and it was getting close to dinner time. But something told me we'd manage a way to open it. We stood staring at the U-Haul.

"Hey, wait a minute," said Barbara. "See how the truck is on a bit of an incline?" It was barely noticeable, but there it was. "Maybe the load is pushing on the door and that's what's preventing it from opening? What if we drive around the block, and as we're coming down the hill, we hit the brakes a couple of times to shift everything away from the door?"

"That's a great idea," I said. "Let's do it."

"First," she replied, "I'm making a drink." She went inside and emerged a bit later with a vodka tonic. As I started the engine, Barbara looked at me and said, "Okay, Mo, do your thing! Just don't spill my drink."

I smiled and obliged.

"Dear Lord," I began, "Thank you for getting us here safely. Please help us. Please make it so that we can open this door. We ask this in Christ's name. Amen."

Barbara raised her glass, "Amen!"

We pulled cautiously out of our parking space and took a right onto the main road. At the next left, we turned and made our way up a hill, then wound around to the left two more times and found ourselves on a steep descent. All the way down the block, I'd drive a little then abruptly hit the brakes as Barbara watched to make sure her drink didn't spill. And we giggled.

"I hope no one is watching out their windows!" I said.

We laughed our way back to my new place and parked across the street, this time facing the opposite direction so the hood of the truck faced the slight downhill. Barbara and I looked at each other. "Please, Lord," I said.

When we got out and walked around to the back of the U-Haul, our jaws dropped. The unlocked door had rolled open, 100%. We looked at each other, momentarily speechless. A pleasant shiver passed over us.

"Praise the Lord!" I said.

"Well, you know, laws of physics," added Barbara.

I just smiled. "Yeah, and I know who created those laws."

My Narnia

2005

From childhood, I have been able to lose myself in a good book. Of course, part of what you do when you lose yourself in a good book is to find yourself there too. I'm telling you, I owe C. S. Lewis a debt, and when I get to Heaven, I'll join the line of other grateful kids queuing up to tell him what his series, *The Chronicles of Narnia*, meant to them. I suspect we won't have to say a word; he'll get it.

Those tales of Lucy, Edmund, Peter and Susan lit a candle of hope in me. Or perhaps they fanned a tiny flame that is there in all of us, although it may be hidden under ruin and ash. It was a time when I felt tiny and wretched and incapable, and the world I could see contained much that was painful, confusing, even vile. I couldn't make sense of it all. But when C.S. Lewis took me to Narnia, I saw a place where the difference between good and evil was clear, and in spite of overwhelming odds –

even when evil reigned for long periods of time and it seemed would prevail - the good ultimately triumphed.

In Narnia, ordinary kids became queens and kings, and it truly was a process of becoming: They had to learn from their mistakes along the way. The children's actions mattered. Their lives held significance.

And then there was Aslan. O, Aslan! He was trustworthy beyond any doubt, loving, playful, and personal. Actually, the children did sometimes doubt his trustworthiness, but he always proved faithful. That was a relief.

When I was nine or ten, I composed a letter to C.S. Lewis to thank him for writing those books. This would have been in the mid-1970s, and I didn't realize he'd died more than a decade ago. I didn't know where to start. The words seemed inadequate. I'm reminded of that inadequacy even now.

Traveling Mercies

2004

I've begun reading Anne Lamott's *Traveling Mercies*. Reading Anne Lamott helps me to find the courage to write with honesty, though I am a different sort of person and a different sort of writer than Anne. I remember Robert, my younger brother, telling me often, "You're sooo serious!" And so I am. Or maybe there's an element of calm, like my wise oldest brother Al observed in his most recent email to me. I hope that is true. And then there are all of these brothers and sisters to write about. I feel like I need to begin with a genealogy before I begin to write, like Tolkien providing the map of Middle Earth.

I self-observe so much. I like to say I'm this or I'm that. Don't good writers describe something and let the reader decide? What does a writer do who has lived so much of life in her head? Am I to be ashamed of that and try to overcome it with dazzling descriptions of sensory experiences?

And what do I do with this propensity to get drawn into conversation with God about so many things? That's what happens when I'm honest most of the time. Before long, I'm talking to God about it, because he's the measure of honesty in the first place. Will I put people off and offend them with God talk? Will they find me ludicrous?

I guess I need to think about who my audience might be. That is hard though. I don't want to write for an audience, I want to write for the sake of the truth. But one reason to write is simply to bear witness. Maybe that is more to the point of what I am doing. God has done something in my life. I do want to bear witness to that. God knows my heart as I write, so I don't have to stop every five seconds to say thank you or say his name, JESUS. Yes, he is my Lord and my Savior!

How do I write now with this cancer?

Realistically I probably have a couple more years to live. Yes, I know that God may grant me longer, but someone with my diagnosis usually lives 18-24 months from the diagnosis, which I received about 12 months ago. So I'm assuming I'll live longer than that, and I'll set that thought aside.

What I will write about is this past week. I had my third round of chemotherapy on Friday; I sat in the chemo room for more than seven hours and felt fortunate to be able to help calm the fears of a woman, her husband, and their son during her first round of chemo. She came into the room looking like a skittish stray kitten, the kind that barely peeks out from behind the garbage bin, and you know it just wants to relax with the bowl of milk you are offering. You also know it might lash out wildly at you with its claws, scared, stunned, and angry. By the time she and her family left, after talking with me and an older couple, she and her husband were laughing and lingering in the room, having found some peace there, and were now reluctant to leave for the gloom of their home.

Then Saturday was a good day. I was able to focus on the reading I needed to do for my graduate studies. I felt peaceful and calm. On Sunday, however, things took a turn for the worse. I vomited shortly after waking and again a few hours later, and over the next couple of days I felt emotionally and spiritually depleted. Drained. Sapped.

It felt like I was empty. And it felt like truth: I am empty. I need God to fill me with his grace. When you go through chemotherapy, you get stripped of some facades.

Today, I am starting to feel more like myself. I'm reading a great book, and I'm about to go outside and sit in the sun of this glorious Vancouver day and indulge in reading for a while longer, before resigning myself to finish the reading for a class I started nearly a year ago. I had to get an extension for that class because, during that semester that I took it, I started dating Steve, visited England with him in the middle of term to attend his brother's wedding and meet his family, became aware of worsening pain in my hip and back, and received a diagnosis of Stage Four breast cancer, which had metastasized to my bones.

I had radiation during exam week, right before Steve and I went to Virginia for the holidays. On our holiday, he asked me to marry him. Our friends helped us plan our February wedding, start to finish, in two and a half weeks. Soon after our wedding, we found out the cancer had spread to my liver.

So I just couldn't quite get this course done. All the other coursework I started is finished, and I'm determined to get this one done this summer, in between chemotherapy, radiation, bone strengthening IVs and fat-needle cement shots into my spine. I think I can do it, but right now, I need a dose of Anne Lamott. Reading *Traveling Mercies* makes me feel more like myself.

Anne describes spending time with her friend Pammy as her friend drew nearer to death from cancer, and I wonder now how others might feel spending time with me. When Anne writes, one gets the feeling that the time she spent with her much-loved friend was precious in a deep, deep way, charged with an undercurrent of love understood by them both. There have been times lately when I've felt this same undercurrent with my friends, but I miss my own sisters: Mary, Barbara, Monica and Therese.

My Church Family

2004

There is a couple at our church who emigrated from El Salvador twenty-five years ago who have been championing an organized prayer effort for us. They have both spoken up during Sunday worship services, separately and together on several occasions, vehemently insisting that God is calling the people to pray, that he will perform a miracle if we but pray for it. For a couple of weeks, they tried to organize 24-hour prayer, but I don't think it went over very well.

Some people are praying regularly and like the idea of signing up for particular prayer times. One friend took me aside and told me that he and his wife are praying but were not signing up for one of the set time slots. Still others, I suspect, didn't feel called to pray and others probably didn't give it much consideration at all – they have their own stuff going on. I tried to stay out of it. The people at our church have been great, and we really do feel comfortable referring to them as our church family. Steve and I regularly give updates about how we are doing during the sharing times of the service; we feel like we are supposed to keep in close touch with the folks at church, and we're grateful for all the love and support they show us. So I'm not too fussed about whether there is 24-hour prayer or not. I just can't worry too much about it.

Acting In

2004

There is a lot of talk about how people "act out" in reaction to certain things happening to them. For me, it's been more characteristic to "act in," to lash out inside my head, striking out at my own thought-life. That's where my villains lurked.

It has always seemed to me that I wasn't thinking about things properly, was basing conceptions on faulty formulations of ideas. Consequently, I wasn't feeling properly. I had my baseball bat at the ready and whacked away at pieces of worldview that didn't hold up under scrutiny.

I'm not saying I didn't act out in stupid ways. There are times I lived out some theory about life about which I was particularly excited, which I thought to be "true," and lived that way for a while before I took a bat to it. That's all part of it, of course. I did things based on how I was thinking about life, and I was always trying to figure out what the right ways were. It seemed to me that there must be some way to live, some guidelines that made sense, but which eluded me.

I didn't blindly go about living with abandon; my forays into life were meek and gradual, because I had little confidence in the basis of my actions, being possessed of a tendency to become too preoccupied with my thoughts. But that sort of life can keep a body paralyzed, and certainly much of the movement that then happens lacks joy. It is graceless and trudging and halting. Life lived that way feels heavy. Ugh.

But, hey, that is the way it's been for me, and with a little perspective, I can see that there are times it served me well. That sort of hyper-analysis stopped me dead in my tracks a number of times, preventing any number of heinous acts I might otherwise have come to regret. I regretted many things anyway, seeing as I did that they were often the result of my living out of faulty worldviews. There are yucky episodes in my life, acts of stupidity, immorality, cruelty, but most of those episodes didn't last long, since I'd somehow see that I was whacked and so would cease going down that road.

It was a series of walk walk walk, right turn, left turn, keep following the path, looks good, road keeps going, walk walk walk...and then SCREECH! Halt! Big wall in front...SMACK. Fall down on my butt, rub my whacked head. Stand up again. See the wall, backtrack a bit to some prior crossroad, and groggily, gingerly, creep down another direction. Sometimes I'd stubbornly go down the same road again. Some walls left deeper imprints on my head because I had to hit them several times before realizing they wouldn't move for me.

That's the way it was for more than 30 years of my life, until I got to a point where I began to question my mode of living itself. I had always assumed there was a "way" to live that made sense, but all the ways I tried didn't work. I couldn't figure it out. Maybe it couldn't be worked out. Maybe I was going about it all wrong. Maybe it didn't matter so much how I lived. But why, then, the constant conviction that somehow there was a way? If nothing else, I recognized that as true.

Or maybe all this is just so much bunk in my little insecure mind.

My Bald Head

2005

I just put my wig on. I'll wear it before I go outside to sit and read. It is an okay wig, straight, like my real hair, but there is more of it. My real hair is thin and fine, straight and brown, and this wig has more volume and is a dark honey color, with long layers that fall to my neck but clears my shoulders. Steve and I agreed it was better than the longer wigs that look more luxurious and finely styled; this is a bit tousled and more believable as real hair because it not so perfect. I tried on one that had a longer, more striking quality to it and Steve and I both agreed again that I looked quite a bit like my sister Therese. More often than not, her hair looks really good. And when her hair doesn't necessarily look stunning, she always does. I didn't figure I could carry that off every day.

But I'll wear the wig out in the sun because I look better with than without it. You do realize that all that stuff about bald being beautiful (Sinead O'Connor with her perfect scalp and angelic face notwithstanding) is romanticized sap. My bald head is not beautiful. There are red spots, prickly hairs and a funny tan line.

I'm not too keen on sitting out in the sun either, airing my bald head to the sun's rays in the privacy of our backyard or defiantly on a beach full of people. That gradual burn-tan process seems inappropriate for my bald head. Nor does it seem a good idea to slather it with self-tanning lotion. Steve is a former chemical-physics university professor who has warned me about the solvents in nail polish remover, and every time I've considered fake-tanning my scalp, I think of this and reason that allowing chemicals so close to my brain is wrong.

It's not that we avoid the topic of my bald head. I'll make an occasional joke about it, and he still kisses me like he means it when I have nothing on my bald head. But I know it is not so attractive, that an objective sample of randomly selected people would agree that I look better with the wig. A few might think I look okay with a bandana or one of my several hats. Some of my girl friends who both love me and like stylish hats insist I look great, that my eyes stand out, and I try to accept these compliments gracefully, but, for me, the wig is the best option I have for not looking as washed out and depleted as I sometimes feel. It can't hide the fact that I've few eyebrows and even fewer eyelashes left, but it does cover much of my forehead and thus some of the many skin breakouts that are another side effect of the chemotherapy, and which creep me out when I look in the mirror.

Focusing so much on my physical appearance makes me feel guilty, knowing that so many people in the world are suffering in ways far more real than insulted vanity, but I can't help it. I should get rid of the mirrors or decide it doesn't matter, but I'm accustomed to mirrors and to looking a certain way in them, and I think Steve likes looking at me and takes some pleasure in my looking pretty. He'll be back soon from running down to the marina to work on the sailboat, and I like the idea of his enjoying his first glance when he sees me sitting in the backyard. He's dealing with so much right now, and he's only human. I can't do anything about the rectangular discolored patches on my abdomen and back, or the zapped energy during the days following radiation or my inability to be a full first mate on the boat, enough to go it alone on the water for a few days. He takes it all so well most of the time. The least I can do is put the wig on.

Oh Lord I'll Try

2005

I had a vision once, a vision of me quite different than the hairless me I see in the mirror now. It is good to remember it, but another thing entirely to describe it.

Sometime between two and three years ago I was involved in a Bible study with several other women. It was held in the home of a kindhearted woman named Dawn. The neighborhood was lovely, full of well cared-for homes and yards. All of the ladies in the Bible study were married with young children, except for me. I had been divorced for many years, was a relatively new Christian, and only months before had split for good from my live-in boyfriend, having realized once and for all that premarital sex was wrong for me.

On this particular night, I was ambivalent about going to Bible study. Now don't get me wrong, I always enjoyed the time we spent together talking about God, reading the Bible and praying. It usually was a good time for me, and I suspect that's part of why I sometimes had this hesitation about going. This ambivalence crept up on many of these Tuesday afternoons, trying to persuade me to skip the Tuesday night study and do something alone and isolating, like read a book or watch a movie. It had happened enough that I knew the best thing to do was to go to the study.

While there, I found myself reminded of a song I had always loved, "Come Sail Away" by STYX. Is there a song or two in your past that speaks to something deep inside you? That, when it came on the radio, you shushed whoever else was around so you could listen without distraction to the song, letting it wash over you and into your heart? That's the relationship I had with this song. It connected to a deep, elemental longing inside me. And this night at the study, I was reminded of the role this song played in my life, with its themes of sailing, freedom and faith in the face of uncertainty.

The largely unarticulated hope that welled up in me when I heard this song was to escape with that trustworthy captain. And a sense of trying, oh Lord, always trying, to carry on.

On this particular night, I realized that it was Jesus who sang out to me from this song. I know that may sound strange, and I don't know how God manages to work this stuff out, but all I can say is that I knew then that God had used this song in my life to comfort me and connect with that longing for him that existed deep in my heart. He called to me from the song, and somehow, it helped keep my hope alive, reminding me of a better possible reality. I felt grateful that God would come to me in that way. It helped me to look back on my life and see how God was there, reaching out, in so many circumstances and in so many ways.

As I got in my car to drive home, I realized I had the STYX CD in the car with me, so I put on "Come Sail Away." It was raining torrentially as I pulled out of the driveway and began to listen.

The next thing I knew, a huge sadness welled up inside me, and I began to cry. Sensing that the Spirit was purging me of the grief and despair connected to years of unmet needs and woundings, I allowed the tears to come, crying harder and harder until I considered pulling over to the side of the road. Then, in the blink of an eye, something totally unexpected occurred.

I received a vision. It's the only time I've ever had one, but "vision" is the only way I know how to describe what happened. It was as if I saw it with my heart. And what I saw with my heart as I drove along in the rain sobbing, was of me dressed in a beautiful white wedding gown. I was a bride, fresh and clean and dressed in purest white, with a white veil covering my face. Beside me stood Jesus. I didn't see his face, but I knew it was him. He bent toward me and gently lifted my veil so he could look at my face.

That's it. I gasped aloud there in the car, blown away by the fact that Jesus would want to look so closely at my face. Do you get it? His perfect holiness desired to look at me. I was amazed.

In that moment, I understood that God was telling me I was made totally new, totally pure, through Christ. God could look me in the face because I had been purified. And because that was true, I could let go of all the sadness and fear. My sorrowful sobbing changed to that of relief and gratitude, and I gradually calmed down and listened to the song with new ears.

I no longer feel like I'm desperately trying to carry on, even though I'm staring at the likelihood that my life will be shorter than I once expected. Steve and I have an actual sailboat now, and I can remember all of this while we're out on the water. Steve is the captain on our boat, and God is the captain of my life, and I do believe that I'm free. Maybe that sounds corny or preposterous or fundamentalist. But it's the truth.

A Turning Point

2004

I finally called my friend Diana, who lives outside Philadelphia with her husband. Diana is 6'1", fit and naturally blonde, and when we used to run together around the streets of Washington, D.C., heads would turn in her direction. But one of the things that is so great about Diana is that she doesn't have anything near the stereotypical persona of a gorgeous girl. She's unselfconscious, smart but goofy in the best of ways. Diana tells me how much she has missed hearing my voice, and it was so nice to talk with her again. I updated her on all of my treatment news and stayed on the phone long enough to get beyond that to some news of her, her husband, their jobs, their new home.

She asked about Steve: Was he good to me? Diana and I worked together in D.C., and she was my friend and confidante through a pretty interesting time in my life, when I was trying to figure out if my then-boyfriend was a good guy or a good liar, and when it became quite clear that he was the latter.

What a ride that was. I'm trying to think of a way of telling the story without going through all the sordid details, in part because they are tedious and I'm impatient, and in part because the ugliness is something I'm not sure I want to recall in detail. But there was also some divine assistance extended to me during it all. To give that the attention it deserves, I think you need a little background.

This boyfriend and I were living together the weekend I went away to a women's retreat with my sister, Therese, and realized that Jesus was in fact real. I had been feeling, for a long time, that I was missing a spiritual side to my life.

My siblings agreed that it would be a good thing for me to get married, and my sister Monica introduced me to D., a colleague from her workplace. He and I began to date. My life seemed to be improving. Work was going fine. I was developing closer relationships with my sisters and brothers and getting to know their children better. I felt more connected to them than I had for a long time.

D. and I seemed to get along well. We spent a good amount of time together and had some common interests, especially being outdoors, camping, canoeing, running and other sports. But he wasn't a sailor, and that interest shortly went by the wayside.

My life seemed to be shaping up. In honest moments, however, I had misgivings about my relationship with D. Primarily, I was concerned about the differences in our values and views about God. Although I had stopped trying to figure out ultimate meanings, there were some things about which I felt certain. I had a strong conviction that God existed and that he was good. I had a strong conviction that how I lived my life mattered, and that a big part of living right involved being in loving relationships with others.

I suspected that we people were somehow interconnected and that our actions truly did impact one another. I saw that we have a propensity toward selfishness and came to believe that living for oneself alone was morally wrong. I saw that each of us has the capacity for great evil; that perhaps there was no evil act that a person was incapable of committing given certain circumstances. Therefore, although I was no longer actively pursuing spiritual truth, these convictions held fast, and it bothered me that D. didn't seem to care much about any of it. God wasn't relevant in his life. He neither disbelieved in God nor believed in him. And, in my honest moments, I had to see that D. wasn't very kind-hearted. He seemed good to me, but not always to others. I'd think a little about these things, and then just put them aside.

They would keep resurfacing, however, in a quiet, non-insistent way. I could not help but notice that I felt particularly empty on Sundays. I thought about going to church; I had gone to a Catholic church in my neighborhood in Brooklyn sometimes. But I didn't know where to go, and D. wasn't interested. I didn't want to rock the boat in our relationship. Fortunately, there were others with whom I was close, especially my sisters.

Therese, as I mentioned, had become a Christian years earlier, and she was quite active within her church. It had been clear to me for years that she was sincere in her faith. She had changed dramatically in how she lived her life and interacted with people. She was consistent in giving Jesus credit for the changes in her life, but she didn't preach about him to me. We both recognized in each other a desire to know God. And while she did not preach, it was also clear that she believed in the moral teachings of the Bible, and my lifestyle was contrary to some of them. She didn't seem to look down on me, however, so our relationship grew stronger.

Her faith made me curious, but I couldn't accept that Jesus was the answer. It didn't make sense to me, so I didn't give it all that much thought. The issues would surface in my brain, and I'd focus my attention elsewhere. More and more, though, our friendship strengthened in me the conviction that God was real and that living in keeping with one's convictions mattered. I could never quite escape from the truth that D. and I differed in this.

It was around that time that I was diagnosed with ductal carcinoma in situ, breast cancer, limited to within the breast tissue. The chances of my having this were extremely rare, given my age, but there it was. I had several surgeries to try to remove the cancerous tissue, but evidence of remaining cancer kept surfacing, so I had to go ahead with a mastectomy. D. reacted to all this news quite calmly and went about trying to take care of me following the surgeries. My family members were upset and worried. I was remarkably calm throughout. Somehow, I had a sense of God's care for me.

It was important to me to deal well with the cancer and not allow it to draw me into too much worry or self-focus. I remember wanting to set a good example; this sort of thing didn't have to consume a person. I was never worried about losing my life. It is not that I thought this definitely would not happen, but I didn't feel afraid because I knew there was a good God. This is the sort of thought process that guided me at the time. I tried to reassure family members and continue to be good to those with whom I had relationships.

This isn't to say that the surgeries were not difficult, especially the mastectomy. The day I awoke in the hospital after surgery I couldn't move at all, and I was afraid and weepy. I had a roommate in the hospital room. Before she checked out later that day, she handed me a little slip of blue paper on which she had written, "Philippians 4:6 'Do not be anxious for anything, but in everything by prayer and supplication and with thanksgiving, make your requests known to God, and the peace that surpasses all understanding will guide your hearts and minds in Christ Jesus.'" I was deeply touched. No one had ever given me a verse of scripture before. I felt peaceful. The verse seemed to me to be true, although I didn't know about the Christ Jesus part. What did that mean?

By this time, D. and I were living together, considering marriage. I was all for it; he assured me that was where we were heading but he wasn't quite ready yet. Then my sister Therese asked me if I wanted to go away with her to a women's retreat with her church. Perhaps I was confident enough in my relationship with D. that I was willing to risk more differences of opinion. We'd had more conversations about God, and he had seemed to soften, as my sense of missing a spiritual life had grown harder to ignore.

It seemed to me that D. and I were doing well. For the first time in many years, I was in a good relationship, or so I thought, but my lack of a spiritual life left me with a pervasive sense of emptiness that our relationship could not fill. I couldn't live my life ignoring what I can only describe as my need for God. In the corners of my mind crouched the dim awareness that my desire for God might mean an end to my relationship with D., but I didn't want to ignore this pull any longer, and so I said yes to Therese's invitation.

That was it: The turning point in my life. As I sat in that little room, listening to an energetic Southern woman in a leopard pantsuit talk about the Old Testament and the New Testament and Jesus, I felt sure I belonged in that room. Suddenly a worldview took shape in my mind that made sense of all my experiences and thoughts over the years of my life. I've said it many times as I've tried to describe what happened to people: It was like every little bit of truth that God had given me over the years, which lay scattered like the pieces of a puzzle, came together to form a picture that made sense in every way. It made sense intellectually, emotionally, and spiritually from my own experience and from witnessing others' lives. Jesus was the way. Suddenly I knew this was true, that he was the truth I'd always looked for and longed for. I felt such relief and love and gratitude. I handed my life over to God and told him to do with it whatever he would, and I meant it.

I was incredibly excited. Therese was incredibly excited. But I knew that I had now to confront what was going on in my relationship with D. It seemed likely that we would not be right for each other and might have to break up. I went home from that weekend willing for this to be the outcome.

What followed was a whole series of events that were very confusing and painful, as D. tried to hold onto our relationship and Satan tried to keep me from faith in Christ. That may sound like a bold or crazy statement to make, but I'm sure that's what was happening.

Suffice it to say that God was going to have his way. I joined a church and became involved in weekly Bible study and daily prayer. I realized how starved I'd been, and I ate up all that I could learn and experience of God, Christ and the Holy Spirit. During several months of turmoil, as I struggled to discern whether to stay or leave D., God showed me that he was guiding me and would care for me.

Finally, God made it very clear that the relationship needed to end. In fact, I found out much more than I'd bargained for, which D. never intended for me to know. He'd been lying to me about a number of things, making it clear that my earlier misgivings were on target. I couldn't blame him for the situation in which I found myself, but I was buffeted in my faith that God was full of grace and compassion. I had great hope.

I moved out of the house we had just bought together. We sold it, and I bought a cute little one-bedroom house within walking distance from my church. It had a front porch and a back porch and enough backyard for a garden. I felt incredibly blessed and spent the next two years in the nicest, safest, most growth-enhancing environment I'd ever experienced. I continued in devotion to God and developed close ties with a Christian community. For the first time in many years, I had friends who shared my spiritual passion. Therese and I grew even closer. My sister Monica, a constant loving and protective presence in my life, seemed open to exploring a relationship with Christ. My brother Stephen had also become a Christian, and my relationship with him and his family deepened. In spite of much encouragement to join a church with a singles group and find a man to marry, instead I trusted my sense that God was telling me to let all that go and trust him. He took away my anxiety about getting married and having children. I was now 33 and I had the peaceful assurance that my life would be purposeful, whether I had my own family or not.

My prior interests in helping people through counseling seemed to resurface in a new, changed way. After a year or so, it seemed God might be leading me into areas discipleship and mentoring. When I felt certain needs arising, God brought someone or something into my life to fill them.

Help Me, Please

2005

Lord, I don't even know what I desire. Right now, I want to feel better but not get better, not live too long. I want to throw in the towel because I feel so poorly able to live well. My hope is in you, my hope for life and my hope for death. You are good. I am yours. You are faithful and won't leave me in this tunnel forever. If I live, you'll show me how. If I die, well then, won't I see you? Show me, please, how to trust in you. Show me, please, how to live.

I remember the vision you gave me, and it has become more precious to me lately as I think my understanding of it is deepening. You gave me a vision of myself in a beautiful white gown, as your bride, Lord Jesus, and you condescended to lift my veil and look into my eyes. You stood beside me as my husband. At the time, I took that to mean I was purified in your sight, cleansed, worthy of a white gown. Now I reflect that it is much more than that: It is a promise from you. You are my bridegroom, who promises to be faithful, to love, cherish, protect and keep me. And so you do. Thank you. I know this is nothing that I deserve, that it is only true because you are who you are. Help me to know you better.

Lord, it is hard to look at myself in the mirror. Help me, please. I look ugly. That is hard for me.

A Big Comfy Chair

2005

I'd like to go home today and curl up with Steve in a big, comfy chair. You know, the oversized kind with soft but sturdy cushions, made for one person. One that can take two if they are cuddling close. It would be well-used, soft, with some sort of throw draping it (probably a gift from my mother or my mothering big sister Mary). Steve and I would just slip in next to each other, limbs tangled, and maybe doze off. We'd be content like that for an hour or so.

But we can't do that. We don't have a big comfy chair like that. We have an old futon on which you have to lean too far back. I end up lying down on it most of the time, and more and more Steve just avoids it. If we do sit on it, we're propped up with pillows behind our backs and behind our heads. Steve most often sits in a functional, mostly comfortable Ikea chair if he's not working at his desk. These days, even when watching movies, he often sits there. I'm on the sofa, lying down.

Even if we had the chair, the reality would be that we couldn't sit in it together in the way I envision. Our bodies simply wouldn't abide it. His back or neck would hurt within the first few minutes, to say nothing of my own back. With his ongoing back troubles and mine due to cancer, cuddling close together just doesn't happen very much. Unless the circumstances are just right and our bodies are positioned just so, it hurts one or the other of us.

Somehow, we aren't too frustrated by this. I think it is because of God's grace. You'd think one or the other of us would become fed up, not being able to be intertwined in comfort on a chair, sofa or even a bed, basking in physical intimacy, but somehow, we're not. Neither of us is resentful; I know, we've talked about it. I check it out with him once in a while, because the fact of no resentment on either of our parts surprises me.

We're thankful that we get to be together. I'm grateful for Steve. I know that he likes the idea of snuggling up close to me. I know he has the heart for it, for me. He loves me and even likes me, and I know he's happy to be sharing his life with me. He'd like to be tangled up with me on a lazy afternoon in a big comfy chair. That knowledge comforts me almost as much as the actual snuggle, as long as we add frequent hugs, hand holding, the occasional long look into each others' eyes – all of which do happen. Oh, and kisses.

So, as I walk home this afternoon feeling a little tired, I think that napping with Steve on that chair would be really nice. Because I know he thinks it would be really nice too; I smile contentedly at the mere thought. And I thank God for Steve.

I'm Okay

2005

Holy Father, as happy and filled with your love as I felt yesterday afternoon during and after church, just as tossed about and distressed did I feel last night as I lay unsleeping next to Steve. So many gripes assailed my mind as Steve's snoring took different tones and degrees of loudness that I became frustrated, and the tears began to flow out.

What were the gripes? Many that sounded justifiable: I miss my sisters; I'm going through chemotherapy and it's a big experience and no one in my family is here to share it with me. I don't have friends here like I have back home, friends who both cry and laugh with me. Steve needs a haircut. I want to write but I don't know what to write – I don't want to hurt my family by any of my writing. I can't sleep. I can't get comfortable. Should I pray for someone? For myself?

So finally I got up and went into the bathroom and let the tears just flow out. All the gripes were confused, fuzzy, unclear. I remembered how blessed the afternoon had felt, how God's spirit had filled the church and reminded me of how connected we all are. I sat in the bathroom a little while, blew my nose a few times (hoping I would not wake Steve), and shortly returned to the bed. The pillow was wet and cold where my tears had sunk into it.

I realized that none of the gripes was truly legitimate – not to the extent to make me so agitated. You reminded me, then, Lord, of your promises. I recalled what I had read in the gospels in preparation for sharing communion in church, what Jesus had been up to the evening of the last supper. How he had taught his disciples, his friends, about the kind of love that leads to serving others, about laying down your life for others, about the first being last. I remembered his laying down his life for us. Jesus did that, and I can't say that I understand all that it means, but I know it means that I am free. That I don't have to be big and strong, that I am made one with he who is the source of all strength. At my very essence, I am okay. Jesus has made me okay. I don't lack anything. I don't need to have anything in particular added to me, because I've already been given everything. Only lies tell me otherwise. What have I been listening to tonight?

I could grasp onto any of the gripes and call them my own if I wanted to, if I wanted to negate what Christ has already done for me. I remembered that lies come with confusion, lack of clarity. That's what all of these things are. They were all temptations. If I take anything away, Lord, from last night in terms of what to do, it is to have more prayer and perhaps find a couple of women to pray with – to reveal how these temptations happen and who can join me in prayer. Thank you, Lord, for that reminder.

Lord, I repent of the grumbling. I refute it, do not take it on. The truth is that in the midst of this cancer, I have time to live well. You have and are providing for me. I thank you for the blessing that is Steve. Lord, I ask you to forgive my selfishness. Keep me humble, Lord. Please show me who to pray with, if that is your will for me. Reveal that to me, Lord. Keep me here, Lord, just where you have placed me and have mercy on me, Lord. Change my heart. I want to be obedient to you. Lord, have mercy.

I think I angered the enemy yesterday by my obedience to you at church, and he came at me hard. Father, I ask for your protection against the evil one. Protect me from all temptation.

To you, Lord, be all power and honor and glory, forever and ever. Amen.

I Think Too Much

2004

Well, Lord, I'm tired. Just back from the doctor, I'm feeling plagued, pressed down, pursued by nagging demons that don't want to let up until I'm feeling dissatisfied. It is not as if the appointment went badly. The chemotherapy is working and after another two rounds of it, I should get a break for a while. I'm just feeling a little whiny. Whiny and ineffectual and wondering what I'm doing with my life.

There's a sense of pressure sometimes. I'm trying to do my best in this life of mine and by those people around me. I guess there's some pressure having a husband, parents, nine brothers and sisters and friends and cancer – all these people feel better if I, too, am feeling good. Don't get me wrong, I'm grateful for them all and the love that is shown me.

What I hate are these demons that hassle me. They can't really touch me, I know. I know that I am safe. But if I let them, they can keep me tied up in knots so that I don't get any decent work done. That's the part that has to stop.

Lord, please give me your strength and your guidance and your protection. I know the pressure doesn't have to be there. I don't have to take it on, even if it makes "sense" given the circumstances. I have to remember the admonition given me by several people who have known me well, "You think too much!" Sometimes thinking just doesn't get me anywhere but knotted up and unable to move.

Praying for Time

2004

I talked to my mother on the phone a couple of days ago and was relieved to hear her sounding upbeat. She's so far away, and she worries, and she sounds best when she feels helpful. On a recent visit, she talked of an article she'd read about a young woman whose breast cancer had spread to her bones and then to her liver, like mine. My mother recalled that the woman was on a particular drug – she thought it started with an H. After a couple of years of being on the drug, the woman was doing fine.

"Herceptin?" I asked. "

Yes, I think so."

"I'm on it," I replied, with much satisfaction.

Mom often tells me of conversations she has with her doctors, who tell her of some patient of theirs who had something similarly life-threatening to the cancer in my body, some of whom are going strong even 12 years later. It is helpful for Mom to tell me about these things, but since I'm not walking around in fear of dying, these stories don't reassure me. I don't really need reassuring. Not about dying.

Yesterday I looked up Herceptin on the internet, and then wondered throughout dinner whether I should tell Steve what I read. People who are candidates for Herceptin are those with aggressive cancers that test positive for HER2, a protein, the presence of which portends a more deadly disease. So it's kind of a mixed bag, and I hope my mother doesn't look up the information for herself on the internet. While Herceptin has proven effective in extending the median time of death from 20 to 25 months, it doesn't make much difference for me in my life's outlook. I am not saying I believe that I'll only live 20 or 25 months, but when I look ahead at my life and ask myself questions about how best to live it, Herceptin doesn't factor in.

The point of my life, now that it may be coming to an imminent end, can't be simply to squeeze a few more months out of it. If, for the sake of argument, I'm going to die in 20 or 25 months, it is still going to be heart-wrenching for those people who love me, and something unforeseeable will be happening to me as well. No matter how you look at it.

Will I get to spend some more time with Steve and my family, the people that I love and belong to more than any others? My parents and my nine siblings: Mary, Barbara, Al, Tim, Monica, Steve, Pat, Therese and Robert? It is hard to imagine not having more time to spend with them and deepen those relationships.

I want to know my nieces and nephews and watch them grow. I want moments of companionship with them, of laughter, of sweetness. Lord, I pray for that time.

An American Thanksgiving in Canada

2003

It was an odd day to have a doctor's appointment: the fourth Thursday in November, Thanksgiving Day, 2003. American Thanksgiving, to be exact, as I am in Vancouver and Canadians have their Thanksgiving in October. Their Thanksgiving lacks much of the hype of its U.S. counterpart. Does anyone do hype quite so well as Americans? Certainly not Canada, the more humble outdoorsy cousin to the flaunt-it-if-you've-got-it America.

Steve and I were having friends over for a traditional American Thanksgiving dinner at his place later in the day. We were cooking the turkey, stuffing, gravy and mashed potatoes, and I was making the cranberry orange bread that we usually had at home in Virginia. I'd farmed out other recipes to various friends who would be joining us. Many of these friends are from other countries where these recipes are anything but traditional, so I got to have a bit of fun.

The recipe for Mom's sweet potato pone, a whipped dish with melted marshmallows layered thickly across the top, went to Heather and Marty. It always got grateful and enthusiastic "Yum! I love Mom's sweet potato pone!" at home. But Marty and Heather are from Northern Ireland, where one just doesn't mix the savory with the sweet, and Heather couldn't quite bring herself to smother the whipped sweet potato mixture with the marshmallows. The sparse, balding layer on top would have elicited a moan of disappointment from the folks at home.

The recipe for my sister Therese's awesome corn pudding – a dish that only has a touch of sweetness - went to a couple from Australia, who assumed the recipe was a variation on cornbread (it isn't). When they couldn't find the exact ingredients they improvised with cornbread in mind, and it turned out entirely differently than expected. Lacking familiarity with these American traditional dishes, our guests enjoyed them just the same.

My English husband distanced himself from the whole recipe affair and committed himself to helping stuff the bird and making the gravy. They do that in England with some regularity, I'm told. But I had an ally in my friend Greg, from Texas, who was pleased to be asked to bring along something that's a favorite of his, because that meant he could bring his family's famous Jello salad. I was delighted because, of course (and Greg agrees), no self-respecting American family holiday gathering is complete without a Jello salad.

I had arrived at Steve's early that morning, and together we'd unpacked the turkey and prepared it for the oven. We needed to get it cooking before the doctor's appointment. It was good to have tasks to do, and we went about them without saying a lot.

"Honey, will you rinse the bird off, I probably shouldn't be lifting it," I said.

"Sure," he replied, and set to rinsing while I tore off some paper towels to dry it. Then I salted and buttered the bird while he turned his attention back to the stuffing mixture on the stove.

"Will you hold that flap of skin open while I spoon in the stuffing?" he asked a few minutes later.

"Um-hmm."

We were glad to be working together on the simple task of filling the cavity of the turkey with as much stuffing as we could. We had just enough time to get all the prepping done and the bird in the oven before we had to set off for my doctor's appointment.

Steve and I had been dating just short of three months, and my serious back pain had begun shortly before that. I'd had nagging lower back pain for a long time. A year? More than a year? I'm not sure. But I remember wondering at it and thinking perhaps I wasn't stretching my muscles enough or exercising enough or perhaps I was getting old. Is this the sort of thing that happens at 36? Does old age begin to creep up on you in your mid-thirties, reach out a mean bony hand and poke at your back? I don't know, so I didn't pay much attention to the aching until mid-August.

It began on the morning I was to drive down to Seattle with a friend, meet up with another friend who would have just completed a triathlon there, and spend a few hours with them before they dropped me at the airport. Then, I'd take a flight to Virginia to visit my family, whom I'd missed with a poignant, lonely ache since I'd arrived in Vancouver.

That morning, I awoke with an odd pain in my neck. It was difficult to turn my head to the right, I noticed as I drove. My neck bugged me the whole day, and instead of getting better, it stayed like that for a number of days into my visit home. Finally, toward the end of my trip, when my homesickness had abated and I noticed that I felt renewed and ready to return to Vancouver, I felt it might be getting better. My sister Barbara and I had returned from a long drive to her place. I carried my heavy suitcase up the two flights of stairs to her guest room. My back seemed okay, and I thought: Good. Just in time for my return trip to Vancouver the next day.

But the next morning as I was pulling on a pair of jeans, something seemed to give in the middle of my back. I couldn't even reach down to pull on my jeans, much less put my shoes on, without sharp, searing pain. What in the world? Is this what it feels like when your back goes out, I wondered as Barbara tied my shoes. I'd never felt it before. All I know is that Barbara had to do all my heavy lifting for me as we prepared to go to the airport. She looked worried, watching me wince as I put all my stuff together. She hated to see me in pain, didn't much like seeing me off to a plane that would take me 3,000 miles away from her and all my family either. But see me off she did, after placing my luggage safely in the care of the curbside porter at the airport.

It was within a week of my arrival back in Vancouver that Steve and I started dating. Neither of us could have anticipated how quickly events would unfold, certainly not at the beginning of our courtship, nor at the beginning of that Thanksgiving Day.

Strength Solid and Enduring

2005

In all honesty I have to say I have never felt a real sense of urgency about whether I live or die. I have prayed to God about that. Is this sin on my part? Do I not value my life appropriately or care enough about the people who love me and whom I love? Does my outlook need to be changed? "If so, please change it Lord," I have said.

Instead, I feel at peace. I am Okay and Safe in the most ultimate of ways, through Christ Jesus. Death has lost its sting. God loves those I love even more than I do; he will care for them. Shouldn't I rejoice in these things and cease to be afraid? Should I, instead, be in anguish about possibly facing death? But aren't I to believe that God has me in the palm of his hand? Don't I believe that he works all things for good for those that love him? Don't I believe that he works in mysterious ways, and I can't understand everything he's up to? I do believe these things. Then why would it be better for me to want physical healing?

Instead, I feel encouraged to speak up and tell people what he has been showing me during this time. I do not feel discouraged about lack of physical healing. I do not feel that putting my energies in this area is right for me. Perhaps it is right for others, but God is not speaking this to me.

What he is speaking to me about is his sufficiency. When I am suffering physically or emotionally worried, he eventually comes – in many ways – to lift me up. I feel his care all around me: In the prayers of so many people, many of them strangers; in the expressions of love in word and action from my husband Steve, my family and my friends; in his spiritual presence during prayer; while meditating on the Word; when reading other books or driving along in my truck. He is here. No matter what is going on, when I know that he is here, it is enough. He is enough. This is his continual revelation to me. If I were not going through hardships – sufferings that I would have thought needed to be soothed for my world to be "okay," – perhaps I would not understand his sufficiency.

Truly, when I am weak then I am strong. Because feeling strong in myself alone is not real strength but an illusion. When I'm weak, his strength can manifest. His strength is the real thing, solid and enduring.

Men and Women in the Kingdom of God

2006

V ying for position has no place in the kingdom of God. The apostle Paul uses the analogy of "running the race," but I think he's referring to endurance, finishing what we've started. I don't think he's endorsing a competitive spirit. Vying for position is anathema to the Kingdom that Jesus died to offer us.

As a woman, I search my heart before I speak of something that so often has been a "can of worms" for this congregation and for people, Christian and non-Christian alike, down through the ages. What, I ask myself, is my motivation? Who is prompting my words? Am I speaking out of love? I pray for God's lovingkindness to guide me.

I'm reminded of C.S. Lewis's words in *The Problem of Pain*, that love and kindness are not the same. In fact, love, in desiring the highest good for someone or a group of people, doesn't simply wish those people to lead carefree, happy lives, regardless of the manner in which they live. Love, in desiring the highest good, sometimes says or does things that may pain us, in attempting to steer our hearts toward that good.

As far as I can discern, I'm speaking as the Holy Spirit leads me, flawed though I might be in my delivery.

The arena of proper relations between men and women has been one of great personal searching for me. Violence between the sexes is as old as the human race. And by violence, I mean any way of relating – one created being to another – that in some way negates, says "no" to, the full value, the full humanity of the other person. The obvious examples of violence, of course, are acts of covert physical force or sexual coercion, or perhaps a verbal routing. But I maintain that any act of manipulation, however subtle, is an act of violence. Take the act of the serpent in the Garden of Eden. He made suggestions to Eve, twisting God's words but never her arm, to deceive and manipulate her – an act of violence against her, and the man Adam.

We should be a community that actively struggles with this as we try to live out our call from God to be stewards of creation, priestly people. I submit that this is not a sideline issue that we must push away so we can get on with the "real" work of being

God's people. I submit that this is a big part of the redemption that Christ died for.

Paul, in 1 Timothy and 1 Corinthians, speaks against that pendulum swing – women getting a taste of freedom and then an appetite for power. No, says Paul, that is wrong. The Christian way, for both men and women, is service and empowering others to grow and exercise the gifts that God has bestowed upon them.

How many of you men have had the experience of sharing a problem with other men, perhaps receiving helpful feedback from them – then sharing that same problem with your wife, and also receiving good feedback from another perspective? Was it valuable?

Therefore, in excluding women, are our elders' meetings missing helpful voices? If a woman came along possessed of the sorts of gifts we associate with Elders, are Christ's purposes served by excluding her from eldership? Do we really believe God would turn her away?

I am loathe to use the word "empower" because I do not think power is our right focus. Christ came so that we could be forgiven and live in redemptive freedom.

As people, whether man or woman, we should be leading the way.

I Have to Write a Will

2005

I have to write a will. It is a relief to be able to talk openly about it with the ladies at the Women's Life Group.

"It's not that I have much to leave anyone," I explain, looking around the room at the eight of them. "I just want to make things as easy as possible for Steve and my family."

My glance meets understanding nods from heads with hair in various stages of regrowth. Maria across from me with downy newborn wisps appearing above her startlingly blue and intensely tired eyes. Terri beside me looking out beneath halo of tight Little Orphan Annie pin curls.

Taylor, the group facilitator – she's not a terminal cancer patient so her sandy-colored hair is simply shorn short – asks me some staple therapist's question along the lines of, "And how are you doing with all this?" A thought flashes that I'm above this sort of counseling 101 tactic. I ignore it, let it sit there inert. As I start to reply, "I'm doing well," tears sting my eyes.

"It's actually helpful to talk to all of you about it," I continue truthfully, catching the eye of Maggie in a bright auburn wig. I've only just met her and learned a few minutes ago that she sometimes has the urge to bite her oncologist. She smiles sweetly, encouraging me, and I continue. "I talk to Steve and my family about it, but I can just hear in their voices and see in their eyes that they're struggling with all of this. It's so hard for them. If I talk about these sorts of things right now, it might throw them for too much of a loop. You know what I mean."

They do know what I mean, and they give me helpful advice. I'm guessing that all but one of these women have at least ten years on me, and it looks like most have their wills and wishes set down legally on paper already.

"Everyone, not just us, should have a will," Terri reminds us. "Otherwise, the government gets involved and everything takes forever."

"Yeah," says Dee, her voice raspy but fierce. She takes a labored breath and continues, "And you want to make sure..." She pauses to draw more air, "...that everything gets done the way that you want it." Dee has stopped all her medications, including the morphine that eased her pain but left her feeling less like herself, and now every sentence costs her. She is determined to be herself until the end: gutsy, capable, calling the shots no matter how much it hurts. I'm not fooled by her staunch display of control. She breaks my heart.

"Has everyone here made out a will?" asks Taylor.

I don't share Dee's ambition to conduct all my affairs just so, but I suspect that Dee worries about how her eleven-year-old son will cope after she's gone. It's horrendous for a boy to lose his mother, and she can't do anything about it. To this I relate: I hate seeing those I love in pain, but here I am with this cancer, and while I don't blame myself or anyone else for having it, I see those I love in pain now on a regular basis. So far, this is the hardest thing to deal with. There is nothing I can do about it; there is no chance they will escape suffering.

I said to my husband the other day, "I'm really glad that people care about me. I want them to care. I just don't want them to be hurt."

"Don't be daft," Steve replied, and I smiled, glad that I married an Englishman whose ordinary speech patterns tickle me.

Who knows, maybe there's some ultimate good to be had during or on the far side of grief. I know this idea annoys some people, but it may be so. Truth be told, in my not-uncommon moments of introspection, I find it interesting to be living with cancer. At times I'm startled by joy. Regardless, I can't see much point in anyone having to deal with countless picayune details after I die, and there are things I can do to minimize them. So I want to make a will and provide some details of my last wishes. It will spare Steve and my family some trouble.

These ladies have been there.

Maria with the tired eyes volunteers to bring me the name of her attorney, then begins her "check in" with the group.

"I've been through more chemo, on more drugs, than I can even remember," she begins in a quiet, measured voice. "And I don't...I just..." she hesitates, decides, and says in a stronger tone, "I don't feel like fighting anymore."

The room goes still.

Maria's eyes bore into our faces as she turns to us one by one, and she leans forward almost imperceptibly. Her brows arch, eyes widen. It's not defiance I see on her face, but a moment of unguarded hope. Not hope for a cure, but simply that some woman in this room will understand what she is saying. I'm struck anew by the blue of her eyes and their childlike quality as they seem to implore, "Please, can any of you help me to find rest?"

I gaze out the window, over the tops of city streets, toward the skyscrapers of downtown Vancouver as I try to formulate what I'd like to say. Seconds pass: One...two...three...

...four. "It sounds like you are in a depression," begins Bonnie, a kindly cancer veteran in her mid-fifties with surprisingly thick, shoulder-length real hair. She says it tentatively, nodding her head in short little bobs as she looks around the room gauging support.

There's an almost audible collective exhale.

Sensing approval from the group, Bonnie continues, "I'm on antidepressant medication. You might want to talk to your doctor about that."

"Yeah," says Maggie. "I've been on Prozac for two years."

A couple more women weigh in with how their medication has helped boost their moods.

Maria's eyes narrow, and she sinks back a into her seat. Her journey into terminal illness has progressed beyond mine, past the civilized world of wills and attorneys to where even these strong women fear to tread. At least they do not want to tread there today.

Taylor, sensing Maria's withdrawal, responds with sympathy, "There may be things to help you feel better. But right now what you are saying is that you feel tired. Sometimes it's helpful just to allow that."

Maria nods, takes a breath. Bonnie chimes in, "What sorts of things do you enjoy doing?" Maybe it's my imagination but as Maria turns to answer her eyes don't seem quite so blue anymore.

Feeling somehow let down myself, my eyes fall to my lap. My mind wanders. I resolve to write out my last wishes. I have to do it soon.

My gaze returns to the window. I lift my eyes to the mountains that dwarf the green glass building and feel a familiar stirring in my heart.

As the group breaks up and we walk toward the elevators, I hang back and wait for Maria. After half a corridor of silence,

I venture, "I think I know at least a little of what you mean by being tired of fighting." She smiles wryly and nods; I think she believes me. I would like to say more but now is not the time.

It occurs to me then, as we enter the elevator, that the most meaningful thing I have to give anyone is my story. And there it is again: "Write."

It has been growing in me, this desire – perhaps a need – to tell my story. "Write," I keep hearing, in a soundless voice, simple and calm. It doesn't clamber or compete for my attention; it has been easy to ignore. "Write." The voice echoes silently back through my past. I don't know when it began; I don't know where to begin. Several years ago when I was long-divorced and celibate and had stopped panicking about my biological clock, I dreamed I had a baby. The baby's name was Daniel, my father's middle name, and he spoke to me intelligently and in complete sentences. I marveled – complete sentences! "Daniel, can you really talk to me in complete sentences?" I inanely asked the newborn in my dream. With perfect diction, he assured me that he could. The dream's vividness recalled it to memory from time to time, but I didn't get it. I can be a little dense.

Last winter I lay down to rest one afternoon during a retreat to a peaceful house on a quiet island, surrounded by an aura of meditative holiness that both soothed and quickened me. I had been lost in Annie Dillard's *The Writing Life* since I'd arrived the previous evening and plucked it off the living room shelf. I dreamed: A wise little woman with long hair wound in a loose bun delivered the message that I was soon to become pregnant. I awoke and wondered, could this be? I would be remarried in a month. But I took medication that lowered my estrogen and kicked me into a menopausal state, sweating and sleepless. I looked at the book sitting next to me. Finally, it clicked: "Write."

The summer came, and, with it, chemotherapy. Autumn. Winter. Along with the cancer, my desire to write has continued to grow. I wonder, are these birth pangs I feel? I wonder, is it now or never? More and more I hear it. "Write," it simply says, as if it were an offhand remark from an acquaintance at a party, or during a lecture at college, or when the ladies laugh and growl during our Life group. I hear the words of T.S. Eliot, long loved and rediscovered: "We shall not cease from exploration…"

So I write.

Take a Deep Breath

2004

"Take a deep breath. Hold it," instructs the doctor. He speaks slowly in a deliberate soothing tone, using the same words each time. Tranquil indiscriminate New-Age Muzak tinkles in the background.

I guard my inhaled air against any slight escape and take in the plastic bins on the steel shelved gurney a few feet away. Sharpie marked labels read: "Syringes; 2 ccs; 5 ccs; 10 ccs; 25 ccs; 50 ccs." Yikes, that's got to hurt. Is one of them the spring-loaded beauty plunged under my arm – in this very room - at least twenty times during my biopsy last year? I'm glad all I've got to deal with right now is this warm slippery mouse pressing its way over my ribs and abdomen and a moment's mild panic that I might have to exhale before given permission. I grin inwardly at myself. As Therese likes to say, in spite of everything I'm still a "goodie-goodie." I remember laughing with her one afternoon in a parking lot before I left Pennsylvania, seeing the contrast between us exemplified in the two vehicles we approached: My little white Honda next to her big black Ford SUV.

"You can exhale," says the doctor. "Now roll over on your back please."

As I'm turning, I manage a few glimpses of his face. He is Asian, maybe Malaysian, just shy of forty, probably stylish under his white lab coat. Looks like a European-cut shirt framing his thin build.

The computer screen near my right shoulder is no longer visible, but eight feet ahead of me I see a half-dozen plastic slides, the results of the previous ultrasound test, clipped up on backlit whiteboards. They could be a series of pocked, asymmetrical lunar landscapes. What does a healthy liver look like, I wonder? Are the dark spots cancer? I keep my questions to myself, enjoying the quiet atmosphere. Let the man do his job. To the left of the white board is a cartoon printout of a cute furry chick. I grin again; they love cartoons here. There's also a photo of an orca whale, apparently obligatory for medical facilities in British Columbia. I study its massive tail curving gracefully over the surface of the water, allowing myself to be taken with wonder.

He puts the mouse down, leaves me on my side on the examining table, and crosses over to peer at the images. He reads something out of the open chart on the desk below. He comes back, adds more warm goo to the mouse, continues, "Okay.

Take a deep breathe. Hold it," as he retraces the path just under my ribs. It goes on like this for more than three quarters of an hour.

I like this guy. This is my fourth ultrasound test, the second one he's administered. The first two were done in a contracting clinic outside the hospital, but my primary oncologist wasn't convinced. At the other place, the test was over in fifteen minutes. I appreciate the thoroughness of the doctor here. He's focused and mostly silent and only asks me questions pertinent to the task he's performing, spending the rest of the time going over and over my midsection with the mouse, staring intently at the images appearing on the screen, telling me to breathe and exhale. His demeanor instills confidence, and he brought me a warm blanket before we started.

"OK, we're finished," the doctor says, "Wait here a few minutes."

He walks out of the room, comes back in shortly with several new films. He takes down a few of the old films and puts up the new ones, studies them.

"Have you had a CT scan of your liver?"

"No. Just ultrasound."

"Have you had a bone scan?"

"Yes," I reply, wondering what he's fishing for. "I've had a couple of them. We know the cancer is in my bones. Most of my spine has been radiated. I'm starting to wonder about my ribs."

He seems satisfied, so I stop here. I make a mental note to call my radiation oncologist.

"We're finished."

"Thank you," I tell him as I leave the room. He nods, invisible wheels turning over in his head as he looks at me. I know the drill. He will synthesize his findings in a written report. My primary oncologist will have the results in four days. I'll read it during my next visit. Steve and I will decide if it's feasible to book that trip to Mexico.

The doctor goes off through the back door to fetch his next patient. I walk out, change back into my shirt, humming that tinkling melody.

They can make you smile if you allow them: The warm blankets, the corny cartoons, prints of gigantic orcas, memories of sisters, doctors deep in concentration.

An Army of Aches and Pains

2005

I have an army of minor aches and pains in my body these days: A dull throb across my chest, a little stab on a lower right rib, soreness in my hip joints that radiates down my quadriceps, several tender spots along my spine. The cancer has pitched tents in strategic locations, is sending out troops and gathering reinforcements. The duvet rustles in the dark as I flop – a bit gingerly, which isn't very satisfying – from my back to my side. I lie still and make sure I haven't made anything worse by moving into this position, before straining my neck to take in the time: 3:15 am.

I hear the drone of a car as it drives by the house, then the distant snore of our landlady, sleeping soundly one floor above us. I listen to make sure Steve - an arm's length from me in our king-size bed - is breathing. He's only an intermittent snorer, although every so often his intake of air is so violent that I'm tempted to turn on the light to make sure he hasn't engulfed his entire face. At those times, if he doesn't wake himself up and I can't take it anymore, I kick at the duvet so it will crinkle loudly, and he'll stir and stop for a while. But tonight, he's quiet. It's not his fault that I'm so often restless nowadays when I should be sleeping.

No, I blame it on induced menopause. That, and a system-shocking barrage of medication culminating in chemotherapy – the big guns – injected and ingested into my body since we learned a year and a half ago that this breast cancer had metastasized first to my bones and then to my liver.

I can't complain too much. A couple of poor sleeping years out of thirty-eight aren't so bad. I used to be a really good sleeper. It was my specialty; I'm known for it in family annals. My brother Pat is known for his eating gusto. Self-dubbed "The Eater," he always cleaned his plate and several more besides. He was a compassionate eater too, once gobbling down Grandma's burnt chocolate pudding while the rest of us gagged because he didn't want to hurt her feelings. Mary, my eldest sister, will always be remembered both for her fierce babysitting tactics during adolescence ("You will stand in that corner and hold that broom straight out in front of you until Mom and Dad get home."), and her exceptionally generous heart in adulthood. She's a maniacal gift-giver; I've had to remind her that Steve and I have a very small apartment.

Me? Well, in addition to sweeping changes that reshape my life every five years or so, causing various family and friends to shake their heads in a mixture of puzzled amusement and worry, I'm known for sleeping. On airplanes, I'd be out before the safety video ended. People were jealous. I traveled to Europe once with Monica and my parents and they tried admirably to control their envy. When I nodded off in Heathrow on stiff-backed benches it was the last straw for Monica. Laughing, she badgered me awake, "You can't sleep! It's not fair! Stay awake and talk to us!"

I sigh – ah, the days – and flip again onto my back. It really isn't that bad. It's not as if I have a schedule that demands I rise at first light. I can sleep in, and by morning I tend to be more relaxed and comfortable. It's just that the purpose of nighttime seems to have changed from rest to wondering. Something's afoot. Reading Internet information sites that quote average life expectancy for someone in my shoes at eighteen to twenty-four months – and now eighteen months have passed – can make a girl think. Nighttime affords lots of time. Its quiet is long and uninterrupted, allowing my thoughts to steep in the darkness like tea in hot water, swirling and taking on deeper hues.

What has happened to Maria with the tired eyes? She died on Friday. Taylor sent around an email, and I was shocked by the picture that was attached. It showed a Maria I never met: A confident, happy and plump woman of fifty, unlike the Maria I sat beside at lunch a month ago, listening to her indict the vicious nuns that ran her primary school. She was a much thinner, balder woman, her face all eyes like a mischievous but tormented little girl.

I inhale, drawing on my counseling days (you can't be anxious and breathe calmly at the same time), and see her eyes, feel the pool that springs up behind my own and exhale long and deliberately. I want to stay calm, to remain in this peaceful place even while my heart goes out to Maria, wherever she is. Has she found the rest that she wanted? Oh, God, I hope so. Lord, have mercy. Please, have mercy on us all.

I place a period on the end of the plea and Maria's eyes recede as I drift elsewhere. I'm surprised I don't feel despair. An acquaintance at school today told me he and his family pray for me and Steve almost every day. I don't even know this guy, and Steve knows him only a little. People keep telling us they are praying, and I think I feel it. My thoughts feel supported and protected, the tea held in a sturdy mug. They don't ooze out in a thousand potentially perilous directions, not anymore.

We Need a Vacation

2004

Steve and I sit beside each other, pillows propped behind us to cushion our bad backs against the wooden pews. What a pair we are, my spine riddled with cancer, his with God-knows-what that keeps causing him trouble and repeated visits to the physiotherapist. Not much more than a year ago – two days before we said our vows to each other, here in this unassuming little church – he'd thrown it out painfully. He couldn't even turn his head. He visited the physio three times in those two days, the last time at 7:30 a.m. the day of our wedding. His back, in one way or another, has been causing him trouble off and on ever since.

The treatment the morning of our wedding seemed to help, and he made it through the day feeling strong. Maybe his excitement and the utter joy that filled this room, little more than a year ago, had something to do with it. We had both soared through the day, buoyed by the outpouring of love and elbow grease from our friends over the prior two and a half weeks – our entire wedding planning period. The plain, white-painted wooden entryway was transformed into a graceful arch of ivy and ivory ribbon; candles lined the windows twenty feet above the pews; luscious red roses burst from three huge homemade arrangements at the front, set off by smaller flowers in subtle pinks and whites. In the side room, Monica and Therese fussed over me, smoothing my hair and soothing my nerves. When it was almost time, they helped me into my wedding gown and even lifted my very non-Cinderella-like size ten feet into pretty white shoes and refreshed my lipstick. A few minutes later, my brother, Stephen, rapped softly at the door and I walked out into the back of the church on his arm.

My father didn't make it to our wedding, afraid as he is of flying during these days of moderate, slowly progressing dementia. But we knew we had his blessing. He'd been weak with gratitude the day that Steve respectfully made our intentions known to Dad during a private man-to-man moment. We were at my parents' home for the Christmas holidays. Later, after Steve and Dad came back inside from their little chat, Dad approached me and gently took both of my hands and clasped them between his own. Choked by emotion, he struggled to speak, leaning toward me slightly as we stood, face-to-face.

"Thank you," he said, red-eyed and trembling, "for being so good to me."

"You're welcome," I said.

So I'd decided I'd walk down the aisle escorted by the eldest brother able to attend our wedding, which turned out to be Stephen. It was fitting, since we'd grown so close during the several years since he rescued me from New York City. Responding to my cry for help, he'd swept into town in a rented orange chariot, loaded me and my few worldly belongings into it, and whisked me away to our hometown. When I moved out here to Vancouver and six months later took this Brit home to meet the family, Stephen took a quick shine to Steve. My entire family did, seeing how kind he was to me and what a sly competitive so-and-so he was. "I play a little pool," he'd said on New Year's Eve at Therese and Jeff's, then wiped the table with them.

Now, it was all Stephen and I could do to keep from blubbering our way down the aisle as all eyes turned our way. Steve only stole one peek, preferring to keep to the English tradition in which the groom waits stalwartly for his bride, eyes to front. By the time I made it to him, I was shaking ever so slightly. The tremor ceased when the first hymn began, and I heard the church full of people – local friends and family who'd flown in with so little notice – rise up and declare, "My God, how great thou art!" The whole day rang out with that goodness, the amazing sense of rightness I'd witnessed so many times before that boldly underscored the time Steve and I spent together. I had kept my grubby little paws off the controls this time and had watched with humble delight as God brought the two of us together.

As I bring my mind back to today, sitting next to Steve a year later, I try to listen to Mark, our pastor, as he teaches of Jesus' Sermon on the Mount. Soon something begins to niggle at me. God's spirit is up to something. I give an internal nod of consent: Go ahead, Lord, show me what I need to see. And I'm reminded of myself seated at Steve's computer a few days earlier. I sat there for hours, eating poorly throughout the day and ignoring the "Honey, don't you think you should give it a rest for a little while" vibes Steve was sending my way. I kept surfing for the perfect, warm-water spot in Mexico where Steve and I could go to unwind for a little while at the end of term, when Steve's classes are over.

Listening to Mark's voice and aware of a poke at my conscience, I wonder: Is it wrong to spend the money to go to Mexico?

Mark is preaching against striving for material wealth. We've all taken a few minutes, in small groups, to talk about it, and now as Mark continues, I stop listening. Steve and I may not be the best budgeters in the world, and surely we have more than the bare necessities, but I don't think money is the issue. That's not what's bugging me. But sitting there surfing the web so stubbornly, long after my back began to ache: that was weird, a little obsessive. When I thought I'd found just the right place for our holiday, Steve had taken a good look himself and then voiced concern that there was a steep walk from the beach to the hotel, and no elevators inside the hotel. Might that be a little too much, too hard on us, especially me?

"I can walk fine. It'll be no big deal," I'd said, irritated that he didn't show more enthusiasm, pretending I didn't hear the defensive edge in my voice. I allowed myself to hear it now.

And what about this onslaught – no, surely they can't really amount to an onslaught – of physical symptoms in my body over the past couple weeks? Steve hadn't pressed the issue; he dropped his protest about the steep walk at the hotel. But he'd heard me comment about my left hip; he'd seen my gait slow and my walks shorten. Still, I stayed at the computer, inquiring about availability. The next day, it seemed my long hours had paid off. I decided the place was perfect. It was available during the time we wanted. All we had to do now was book it – probably on Monday.

"Am I worrying unnecessarily?" I wonder, shifting on the bench, not listening now to Mark at all. I hear a seductive suggestion: Just have faith. But no, no, no, that is not it. It is not a lack of faith to notice and admit that my body is hurting and that it is getting worse. An ostrich with her head in the sand is bound to get burned in Mexico.

I begin to cry now and just allow all the thoughts and images to work away in my mind. I think of Steve and me here, saying our vows. And then: We didn't really have much of a honeymoon. Steve needs this vacation. We both do. It will give him good memories in the future of a time when we explored a new place together. Maybe Steve will be able to relax, and it will carry him for a while. Maybe he'll see God blessing us in the gentle warmth of Caribbean waters. I want to feel warm water. It's too doggone cold here.

What about the pain in my chest? What if it spreads to my lungs? Maybe Steve will begin to view our situation differently when we come back. Maybe he'll be able to see more to rejoice in and less to be sad about. However, if I start chemo soon, maybe I'll live longer. But then Steve doesn't get a vacation. What about quality of life? It will be hard on him not to have a vacation. It will be hard on him not to have me. "Trust God; follow Christ," Mark is saying. Our vows of a year ago reverberate in my mind: For richer or for poorer; in sickness and in health.

My shoulders slump and I hear a short sentence begin to repeat itself over and over in my head, "I can't." I go ahead and cry.

One of the things I like about Steve: He brings two handkerchiefs to church. He reaches into his pocket now and hands me the clean one. I dab at my eyes and blow my nose and lean over to whisper in his ear, "Can we pray with Mark after the service?"

"Sure," he says.

I'm still a little muddled as the three of us sit down to pray, and I offer only the briefest explanation of what's going on. It's not enough of a roadmap for Steve to be comfortable.

"I'd sort of like to know more where we're going," he says.

I shake my head, "I'm not sure. It'll be better for me just to jump in and pray from my heart. I need to get out of my head."

He nods his assent. Mark nods too, and we bow our heads. We ask for God's guidance.

"I keep hearing 'I can't,'" I say, and then just blurt it all out. I talk about the trip to Mexico, briefly touching on money issues, our rationale for taking the vacation. I mention wanting to write, being afraid of getting too sick to continue. I talk about wanting to be content, wanting to be obedient, wanting Steve to be happy. It all comes out in a rush, but as I say it aloud, my prayer begins to focus.

"My body is feeling worse. I don't trust going away. I haven't wanted to admit it. I've been stubborn about it, wanted to make sure it happened. I've been pretending I'm not getting worse quickly, pretending we can go away to Mexico and then I can visit my family and then chemo will start. I pretended it will all work out just the way I want it. You need to have a holiday – and I want one too. You are used to nice holidays, and you haven't had one in a long time. But I'm getting worse. I feel it. It's happening fast. I haven't wanted to admit it, but it's true."

We are all quiet for a few seconds, but none of us moves. We don't feel done yet. Steve breaks the silence.

"The thing I'm hearing," he says, softly but clearly, "is you want to take care of me."

Bingo.

A sob catches in my throat, and I nod, sticking out my lower lip in a pout just for emphasis. I lay my head against his chest.

"You can't do that," he says.

We all sit there for a minute while that sinks in. That's the crux of it, really. But "taking care of" can just be a pretty way of saying "control."

"I know it's not my job. But come on, not even a little bit? Can't I just make sure everything for you is just right? Don't I get to be super-wife? I know what's best for you. And can't you respond to everything that's going on just the way that I think you should? Can't you see all of this the way I think you should see it, and not get too worried or depressed? Can't you do it all just the way I want you to?" I feel like the hysterical Cathy in the comic strip.

Mark grunts his understanding but doesn't say anything. Steve holds my hand.

I know. It's ridiculous and I'm exhausted and I give up. Here I am with these grabby, grubby paws again. Okay, God, he's yours. I'm sorry. Thanks for speaking up. Help me to keep remembering that your arrangements are so much better than mine. Help me.

We walk out of the church, and head back to our car. Today is Steve's birthday and we've decided to go get lunch and maybe find him a new pair of jeans. I scouted out a shop recently when Barbara was visiting. He's very picky about his jeans. No dull Levis.

In the car I nudge his arm away from the middle console. "Do you mind if I put on a CD?" I ask.

He hesitates just a fraction of a second, knowing I'm going for some sappy worship song because my heart's been stretched this morning, and says "Sure."

I am looking for something like that, but then I see our Tom Petty CD – not what one would call Christian Rock – and as the title of the first track catches my eye, I grin inwardly. Subtly shielding the disk from Steve's view, I slide it into the player.

Tom begins, "She's a good girl; loves her Mama..." and I watch with great satisfaction as a slow smile rises up to fill Steve's face, like a lazy summer sunrise. Who needs Mexico? He's got great crinkles at the corners of his eyes.

We drive downtown, replaying the same song several times, hollering out together the verse containing the words of the song's title. We sing along to Tom Petty with abandon and – oddly – unmitigated joy: "Now I'm FREE! Free fallin'!"

A Wild Place

2005

The heart catheterization ward connects two hallways, apparently, as a steady stream of hospital personnel crosses from one to the other, like actors moving stage left to stage right. My bed is front row center.

A disheveled orderly walks by for the third time. First, she marched across the stage as if late for an appointment, her lip jutting out almost as far as her belly. Next, she came from the same direction: same gait, same belly, same expressionless face, arms laden with files. Here she is again, ridiculous in rubber gloves and a plastic cap. How did she get back to stage left so fast? I imagine a director with a knack for comic timing hiding in the wings, having just given a little push with a whisper, "There's your cue!"

What a wild place this is.

A white-haired, pot-bellied paramedic swaggers onto the ward, stops. He glances around. Perhaps because I'm the only patient here with eyes open, he stops in front of me.

"We picking you up?" he asks, inclining his head and raising his eyebrows in mock flirtation.

"No, I'm afraid not," I say, hitching my thumb toward the elderly man in the stall to my right.

A second paramedic, white-haired and wiry, walks in and joins his partner. "She the one?" he parrots. Paramedic One shakes his head sadly.

"Naw, here's our guy," he says, emphasizing his last word.

Both turn their attention toward their charge and reach for the next joke. Alice, one of two nurses frenetically working the ward, sets them up: "Make sure you bring his bag of clothes."

"Rats," says Paramedic One, looking at me and jabbing his partner in the ribs, "Women's underwear sells for more."

Alice and I grin obligingly at their practiced comic routine.

I am grateful for the distraction. One more thing to break up the waiting. I can't avoid fixating on the wall clock to the left. It's one o'clock, two hours since I changed into this backless gown, settled into the bed in stall number five, and began taking in the show. That was after arriving at this massive general hospital at ten o'clock, only to be told the doctors were backed up, to go away and return at eleven.

Unlike the serenity of the cancer center where I usually go for testing and treatment, this place hops. It is also short-staffed, with two nurses tending to the patients in the six beds plus whatever unseen duties periodically draw them behind the scenes. Jack, the charge nurse, pretends to be exasperated at the pace but, I suspect, actually enjoys the adrenaline. Alice works on another ward but is here to help Jack out. They're snowboarding buddies, she told me when she sloppily started my IV. I bled all over the white sheet. "Oops," she said, "I'm making a mess."

I barely care. That was the last digging needle for a while, maybe forever. Once they finally wheel me into the operating room, the doctor will install a port in my chest to provide the drugs easy access to my veins. The reasons for the installation are two-fold: My veins are getting tired and thin from the last twenty months of treatment and the next chemo drug I'm about to start is vicious, it burns out little veins. Once the device is in, a quick jab to the center of it does the trick. No more nurses frustrated by my rolling veins. No more silent prayers: Please, let her get it in the first time. A particularly kind-hearted nurse at the cancer hospital, who cringes every time she has to start an IV, yesterday blurted out, "Oh, thank God!" when I told her I was getting a port. Then her face flushed, and she apologized. "That's okay," I said, glad for the momentary break in professionalism that divides practitioner from patient. "I know it's not your favorite part of the job."

Jack hurries past again, and glancing back at me, hollers, "I'll get you that pamphlet to read in a minute." He said the same an hour ago.

"Okay."

What I really want is another blanket. Good grief, it's cold in here. I guess they don't want blood flowing too easily through all these newly implanted devices. But I've decided to wait for a lull before asking Jack or Alice for another blanket.

I do stop Alice, however, to point out that the gentleman in the bed opposite me has begun tugging at the tube running around his face and into his nose. He appears only semi-conscious, and his leg twitches violently. Alice walks over, checks, and motions to me that he's okay, doesn't need the oxygen any longer. I guess leg spasms are common when one has just had a tube run from thigh to heart. Yikes. He opens his eyes at a question from Alice, and I close mine to give him some privacy.

From the nearby lounge, I hear Jack trying to reason with a lady who's irate at having been kept waiting so long. She sounds very angry, pouring out blame on the only one she can. What is blame, I wonder? Why do we want someone to blame when things go wrong? Does it make anything better? Can we then prevail upon the guilty party for positive change? Sometimes. But sometimes a thing's just done and there's no changing it. I hear the nasty edge in the woman's voice in the waiting room. Can blame just mask our desire to hate?

I shudder. I've been that lady, puffing myself up with my rights, vehemently denouncing – or quietly turning an icy back to – those who did me wrong. Could easily be her now, if I gave in to the temptation to grab at what I imagine I deserve. But no, not today. There's nowhere I have to be. There's nothing for me to do in this particular moment. My task is to wait and not be a jerk.

It's interesting how each new hardship tempts me to hatred. It is as if there's this part of me that wants to say, "Okay, this is the last straw. Screw it. Now I know I'm being treated unfairly. I suspected it all along." Then, I'd get to be nasty to other people, pissed off with impunity. After all, I feel so achy and tired, and no one will dare tell me I'm not justified. My friends forgive me easily when I'm short with them. But who doesn't suffer in this world? Suffering is no excuse for being a jerk.

Still, my Self seeks this perverse victory. So I periodically confess, spill my guts to God, meanness and all. It helps.

Can't be much longer now. My eyes move back to the clock. Another half hour has passed. Finally, the doctor walks up, introduces himself and apologizes for the delay. The last procedure – a heart cath, not the simple porta-cath that I'll be getting – had complications.

"I warn you," he says, "it's really cold in the operating room."

Not a Tragedy

2005

"Logic!" said the Professor half to himself. "Why don't they teach logic at these schools? There are only three possibilities. Either your sister is telling lies, or she is mad, or she is telling the truth. You know she doesn't tell lies and it is obvious that she is not mad. For the moment then and unless any further evidence turns up, we must assume that she is telling the truth."

The Professor is reading aloud in his booming, Scottish lilt, from C.S. Lewis's *The Lion, the Witch and the Wardrobe*. He's a very good reader, his voice changing intonation with each character, his whole body tensing with the effort, his legs bouncing on the sofa. Each word is clearly enunciated; he is unselfconscious. I smile, tickled and grateful.

The gathering here was his idea. He suggested it to Steve recently when they met for coffee, knowing what a fan I am of the Narnia books, knowing what a difficult time it has been lately, off and on, for me and for Steve. There's been more chemo for me, a bulging disk for Steve, and a multitude of unanswered questions about the future for both of us. So the Professor sent some emails around, and although it's the last week of regular term, eight of us showed up tonight at Adrian and Russ's place, bedraggled and tired. We feasted on remarkably moist, barely pink pork with rosemary and apples. There were loads of crispy roasted potatoes, a mixed green salad with toasted almonds and mandarin oranges, coarse white and brown bread with lots of butter, and a couple bottles of wine. The Professor bragged about cooking the pork, joked that Russ – whose culinary talent is long-recognized – is preparing him for marriage, teaching him to cook and clean. The meal is delicious. Someone's going to be a lucky girl. But Russ himself brings out the pièce de résistance, a flourless chocolate loaf that slices like thick butter, accompanied by spoonfuls of strawberries and whipped cream. Oh, my.

We linger over the meal for a long time. Greg from Texas tells us about meeting a rattlesnake along a dusty trail in Big Bend National Park.

"Let me show you why it's called Big Bend," he says theatrically, drawing a map of Texas in the air. "For all you U.K. folks, this is Texas. See? It's…"

"BIG," interrupts Steve.

Greg grins, raises his eyebrow at Steve. "Yeah. And the park, see, it's BIG too. And then, down at the bottom of it…"

"...is a BIG BEND," I say.

"Precisely," says Greg, waving his arm in the air like an orchestra conductor.

"I'm from the States. That's how I knew," I laugh.

It's a simple bunch of banter, but it works. Heather, sitting across from Greg, smiles contentedly and takes a sip of wine, her eyes sparkling. She just finished her comprehensive exam today and cooked Steve and me a meal to take home for tomorrow. Marty, the Northern Irishman to my right, Steve's best man at our wedding, laments how his wife keeps giving away his favorite chocolate from home. Russ brings out dessert, serves all the rest of us before handing Marty a plate full of strawberries and cream.

"We ran out of chocolate," he says and we all hoot.

"You people are supposed to be my friends!" Marty says.

We go on like this, bantering and laughing and eating. Finally, around nine-thirty we look at our watches and turn toward the living room to begin reading.

Most of us can't remember the last time we read aloud. It's almost a lost art, this reading aloud, except to very young children, and even then, I suspect it doesn't happen as often or as well as it used to. I think we're missing out. We're all enthralled listening to him talk about how Edmund acted beastly to Lucy, how the Professor supported Lucy's strange tale of a magical land.

"I wonder what they teach them at these schools," says the Professor, scratching his head.

From the sofa to my right, where he lays stretched out resting his back, Steve giggles like a schoolboy. Now that's a soothing sound.

This night is a balm.

It's great to get out and spend a few hours with friends. We have, perhaps, been a little too isolated, nursing our infirmities. These days, I feel a bit like a Munchkin from *The Wizard of Oz*. Not because I've lost more than an inch of height due to spinal compression, the bone settling that occurs in elderly ladies with osteoporosis or late thirty-somethings with spine-eating cancer; I started out a bit over five-foot-seven, so I still tower above the little people. No, as I wake up in the late morning, groggy after a poor sleep, make some coffee, do a few dishes and feel like I need to rest my back again, it's the song the Munchkins sing that runs through my mind and resonates with my life: "We get up at twelve and start to work at one...take an hour for lunch and then at two we're done...."

The range of activities that I do day-to-day has decreased, my experiences funneled over these months so that now I: walk a little, rest; write a little, rest; meet a friend for coffee, rest; go to church and perhaps out for lunch, rest. All this resting can be bad for your health. You can start thinking that the reason for your existence is to feel better, which means the reason for your existence is not for now, but for later. You might then put all your efforts into ensuring that better future, or, more accurately for me, stop making much effort at all until "better" occurs.

Come to think of it, isn't that how so many of us have lived all along? Trying to make life better?

But that leaves one beggar of a question: What if it doesn't get better?

Eugene Peterson, in *Subversive Spirituality*, says that our modern view of death underscores that death: a) is tragic, and b) should be delayed as long as possible. But I don't really feel that way. My most recent angst-filled crying out to God, just last night, was for the exact opposite. "God," I wailed, sitting alone in the park in my car, "I don't want to be here anymore!" When I feel a new ache or pain in my body, a number of feelings stir: fear, sadness, anger, resignation, but also excitement. Excitement? Well, I can't help but wonder if this is the beginning of the end, and if so, I'm not altogether displeased. If my faith in a good, big God is well-founded, my death is not tragic. Maybe it is true that I have to relinquish so much here: dancing lessons with my husband, long runs on the beach, face-to-face contact with my family, holding a baby in my arms. Perhaps it is also true that as I open my hand, God takes it in his own to lead me somewhere. And he will not abandon those I leave behind. Why, then, should it be automatically right to take any drastic measure necessary to delay death?

I feel a little guilty that I think this way, but I'm bucking a defining myth of our day, that the answer lies in staying young and healthy and as physically beautiful as possible. I also don't mean to imply that I lack love for Steve, my family or my friends. I do love them; I care about their lives; I'm committed to caring for them. But Jesus is a reality for me, the truest love of my life. He is the truth of the human heart's desire. So after I cry "I don't want to be here anymore!" a second time, I tell God that, still, I will be here as long as he wants me here. I won't mope around, I won't check out before his whistle blows, only because he's so big and faithful. Pour your love into me, so that I can give it back out. I'm sorry for my complaining. I know I'm safe. Your will be done. Really.

Still, I feel entirely comfortable saying, "No, thank you," when well-meaning, even hurting people who struggle with the fact of my illness offer me potential miracle-cures like consuming nightly bowlfuls of Tibetan Snowflake Fungus.

Steve's animated voice as he begins his turn to read interrupts my reverie.

"Safe?" said Mr. Beaver (speaking to Lucy, Susan and Peter), "Who said anything about safe? 'Course he isn't safe. But he's good."

Mr. Beaver is referring to – shh! – Aslan. This passage used to puzzle me. Intuitively, I knew it was true but wasn't sure what Mr. Beaver meant. How is Aslan unsafe? Now I think I get it. He might lead you up a mountain pass none of your friends wants to follow. He might rebuke you when you're being a selfish, scared little prig. He might cause you to writhe in agony as he tears away your hard, scaly outer shell. And then you are scrubbed pink, new, trembling a little as the fresh air hits your vulnerable skin, refreshing, bracing.

Then again, he might lay out a feast before you, and plop you down in the midst of wonderful, silly, mixed-up, beautiful people who care about you and with whom you almost think you could live forever. Their food strengthens. Their voices soothe.

Still, I'm with Peter, as he replies in the best voice I know – Steve's – to Mr. Beaver's description of Aslan: "I'm longing to see him...even if I do feel frightened when it comes to the point."

Epilogue

Maureen's Farewell

Maureen passed peacefully at home surrounded by her family, with Steve at her side, on December 11, 2006. Before she died, Maureen wrote the following farewell and asked that it be read at her memorial service. Her wish was faithfully carried out before a church packed with family and friends who came from far and wide to celebrate her life.

Steve and I had only just arrived back at my parent's beach house for a brief vacation when I got Taylor's message. The message says that two of the women from the cancer group Taylor facilitates have died. This makes four women I know from the group that have died in the last two months.

Safely alone with my confusion, I lay in bed with thoughts churning. My eyes begin to sting under their lids. I'm struggling.

I want to live in the joy of the truth of who you are, Lord. Help me.

I fall asleep. And I dream.

Steve and I stand face-to-face in a dimly lit drawing room entirely crammed with furniture. Music can be heard – something like a waltz. Steve extends his arm and offers me his hand, inviting me to dance. Warily, I accept, glancing around the crowded room. Surely, there is too much furniture here for dancing. Steve encourages me simply to follow his lead.

I raise my chin up and our eyes meet with my best attempt at a confident smile; his hand gently but firmly presses on the small of my back. We move, cautiously at first. After a hand full of steps I realize we've missed the furniture and I relax. Our eyes focus on each other; to my delight we glide rhythmically, gracefully, step after step.

The room falls away.

There is only me and Steve. Attentive without strain to the smallest nuanced movement of the other, we dance. A shot of peace and joy pierces my heart and radiates outward, filling me. I suddenly know I am dreaming and that this dancing is a snapshot of the deepest foundation of our marriage. It's a taste of pure, undefiled love between man and woman, and it's rich beyond description. It is beyond that which any of us have ever experienced, but perhaps have glimpsed in the best of fleeting moments. Yet the glimpse has been enough to inspire all manner of love song and story and poetry down through the ages. As the dream dance continues for a few more moments, I am deeply awed and deeply grateful.

The scene changes and then several follow quickly, one after the other, bursting with life: friends gathered on deep plush sofas while a strange variety of food – bite-sized chocolates but also bite-sized fish cakes – is passed around on silver trays; two long-haired cats of splendid rainbow patterns startle my eyes and – oddly enough – want to fight each other; misbehaving dogs perform ridiculous, endearing antics for their people like naughty, beloved children. They are all scenes of Life with a capital L. Teeming Life: rich and full and – I don't know why this should surprise me – quirky.

And then, finally, I am in a vast outdoor expanse: a hillside. Throngs of people sit on the ground in front of me, filling my vision as far a my eyes can se. We are all people who have cancer, surrounded also by loved ones. Mom and Barbara sit beside me. We are listening to people tell their stories. My attention is drawn to one particular Asian man, about sixty years old, who sits a couple of yards away. I look into his shining brown eyes into an immense grief, sadness and fear. He's overwhelmed by the cancer he has and by the life he has led.

He is in the middle of his story, and as I listen I am moved and broken and begin to sob.

I hear the utter beauty of the story he's telling. It's a story rife with joy and pain, comedy and tragedy. It's a strange story: there are aspects of it that I understand but many more that are way beyond me. I weep for the sheer immensity of it, in gratitude. Somehow it's my story too. Somehow it is ours. Somehow it is bigger than all of us put together.

I awake, sobbing, my face and pillow wet with tears. When I'm able to think, I realize that God has answered my prayer, and I thank him. I know I have been given a vision of reality: Life, so big it feels like it is – like I am – going to burst. Life as God created it and intended it - the Life for which Jesus died. The promise.

The promise is real – if not the rainbow striped cats.

I feel like I just got to visit the place where fairy tales come from, where great fairy tale writers like George MacDonald and C.S. Lewis get their inspiration .

The next morning I ease out of bed to the smell of coffee brewing in the kitchen.

THE STORMS AS THEY ROLL IN

I settle in next to Mom on the white wicker sofa, and Mom asks,

"Honey, in that group you go to at the cancer hospital...well, they must sometimes....Does anyone ever die?
I figured it must happen. And, honey, I know the answer really, and I know you have told me before. But how is it that you are so peaceful? So hopeful?" she says.

I smile back and feel an energizing surge of excitement.

"Let me tell you about the dream I had last night."
 The truth is, I don't know how to deal with this without God's guidance. That's the truth about this situation and all others. I've learned over and over that I need God's guidance.

I'm comforted knowing God assures us that if we ask him for this wisdom, he will give it to us. So I can rest in that. God knows I'd like to help my family and friends as they live this out.

I long for them to know the thrill and deep satisfaction that comes from relating back and forth with God! There's a whole world that will open up for them that will knock their socks off, in the best possible way.

Lord, I know you love these people more than I ever could.

I pray that you draw them close to you; that they submit and allow themselves to be drawn.

Lord, help me to have patience. Build my character. It needs building. Show me how to live well and – if that is what is happening – to die well.

You do test us, Lord. You strengthen, build character, increase our patience, our love our compassion. Does our journey – in all these areas – go on after we die? If You bring about all this strengthening in us, is it for reasons that transcend our lives – as we know them – here?

Please give me words for others.

I have great hope for all our lives. If God is taking me home to him, he is taking all of you so much closer to him too.

I don't care about mansions or jewels or even chocolate. Stuff (and stuffing myself) never did much for my loneliness. What about all these people in my life now: Steve and my parents; my sisters and brothers; and all my friends; the folks at church? Why have I felt it right to spend so much time trying to share my life with them and sharing in theirs? After so many years of wanting to feel such care and love for others, and to receive it back, what's the point of it all happening now if I'm just going to up and die? It doesn't make sense.

In the darkness, again, I remember God. It helps me to be a little didactic with myself. I remember that he's really really big and really really good. He tells us that we are to love him and each other.

And now I get a little excited, feel my heart flutter and stretch. Relationships matter to him. He's gone through all kinds of trouble to show us that he is for us, that he loves us. He's all about us caring for each other, building strong relationships. It gives me hope that somehow, in some way that I can't fathom, I get to stay involved in the lives of people that I love after I die. It gives me hope that part of worshipping him with all the hosts of the angels and the saints includes caring for the people he cares about. Jesus was crucified, but he was resurrected. And even after he ascended again into heaven, we're told – and I experience it – that he's still alive, active in the lives of people in the world. And if I am to become like him, well then I hope that means somehow my relationships continue and also that I'm infinitely better at loving after I'm in Heaven than I've ever been on Earth. Paul, in 1 Corinthians, likens our current bodies to seeds with potential to blossom into fully-flowered bodies of unimaginable splendor.

Currents of quiet excitement run through me.

Outside in the garden, I hear the two-note trill, a tiny dawn trumpet. The first note is higher than the second; the second sounds longer than the first. This solitary singer always begins the bird's morning sound, "Yoo-hooo...Yoo-who," over and over again, eventually joined by a cacophony of cheerful chatter.

Splendor? I know I can't figure it out with my puny little self-consciousness. Instead I doze in and out of the twitter-patting of the birds for several more hours, automatic, hoping that I get to love these people forever.

Don't forget we can't fathom the depths of God. He is beyond us, but has come down to be with us, out of love and goodness. That is really who he is – really, really big and good – The Source of all love, the Rock. You can count on it.

www.ingramcontent.com/pod-product-compliance
Lightning Source LLC
Chambersburg PA
CBHW060615080526
44585CB00013B/837